A Beginner's Guide To Tracking Dinosaurs

Track Dinosaurs and Discover Truth

Steven Hudgik

Copyright © 2020 Steven Hudgik

all rights reserved. No part of this publication may be reproduced, distributed, or transmitted in any form or by any means, including photocopying, recording, or other electronic or mechanical methods, without the prior written permission of the publisher, except in the case of brief quotations embodied in critical reviews and certain other noncommercial uses permitted by copyright law. For permission requests, write to the author at the following address:

Move to Assurance
P.O. Box 277
Cannon Beach, OR 97110
www.MoveToAssurance.org

ISBN: 9798558825879

SOURCES OF SCRIPTURE QUOTATIONS

Unless otherwise noted, scripture is taken from the NEW AMERICAN STANDARD BIBLE, copyright © 1960, 1963, 1968, 1971, 1972, 1973, 1975, 1977, 1995 by The Lockman Foundation. Used by permission.

KJV – King James Version, public domain

DEDICATION

This book is dedicated to Kornell Nash (1954-2019), a good friend, dinosaur footprint expert, and Christian brother. Kornell was the owner of the Nash Dinosaur Track Quarry in Massachusetts. Over a span of 12 years, he donated dinosaur tracks and many of the other fossils you will see in our museum. Although living on opposite sides of the continent, we spent many hours together talking and sharing experiences. I am particularly thankful for his sharing his experience and knowledge about the Bible, fossils, and dinosaur tracks.

Just as they did not see fit to acknowledge God any longer, God gave them over to a depraved mind, to do those things which are not proper.

~ Romans 1:28

TABLE OF CONTENTS

Introduction	1
1 – Type of Dinosaurs?	5
2 – How Tracks Are Made	11
3 – How Are Dinosaur Tracks Named?	15
4 – Theropod Dinosaur Tracks	21
5 – Ornithopod Dinosaur Tracks	25
6 – Numbering Dinosaur Toes	29
7 – Reading Dinosaur Tracks	31
8 – Can You See The Dinosaur Tracks?	37
9 – Dinosaur Track Mysteries	41
10 – Are Dinosaurs Good To Eat?	49
11 – Preservation of Dinosaur Tracks	55
12 – The Track Evidence	61
13 – Fossil Dinosaur Eggs	67
14 – Dinosaur Egg Evidence	73
15 – False Presuppositions	79
16 – Dinosaur Became Birds?	83
17 – Archaeopteryx	89
18 – Microraptor	93
19 – Dinosaur to Bird: Impossible!	97
20 – Fact Check: Evolution	101
21 – Human Evolution Myths	105
22 – Defining Evolution	109
23 – BBC Gets It Wrong	115
24 – BBC's Proof of Human Evolution	123
25 – Mixed Up Bones	129
26 – Trust Jesus, Not Darwin	135
27 – Who Made God?	141
28 – Who Is Lucy?	147
29 – Is Lucy Saved?	151
30 – The Laetoli Footprints	155
31 – Suppress All Opposition	159
32 – Petrified Trees	163
33 – The Lord Warned Everyone	171
34 – 2nd Peter 2:4-6	175

35 – The Door   179
36 – It Is Finished   183

APPENDICES

A – Ten Questions   185
B – The Nash Dinosaur Track Quarry   189
C – The Age of the Earth   195

    Image Credits   197
    Subject Index   199

Thus says the Lord God,

In the beginning God created the heavens and the earth.

The earth was formless and void, and darkness was over the surface of the deep, and the Spirit of God was moving over the surface of the waters. Then God said, "Let there be light"; and there was light. God saw that the light was good; and God separated the light from the darkness. God called the light day, and the darkness He called night. And there was evening and there was morning, one day.

Then God said, "Let there be an expanse in the midst of the waters, and let it separate the waters from the waters." God made the expanse, and separated the waters which were below the expanse from the waters which were above the expanse; and it was so. God called the expanse heaven. And there was evening and there was morning, a second day.

Then God said, "Let the waters below the heavens be gathered into one place, and let the dry land appear"; and it was so. God called the dry land earth, and the gathering of the waters He called seas; and God saw that it was good.

- Genesis 1:1-10

Beginner's Guide To Tracking Dinosaurs

INTRODUCTION

Would you like to photograph a dinosaur? A real, living dinosaur? What I am talking about is going back in time, tracking down a dinosaur and getting a couple of pictures. Sounds like fun… if you know what you are doing. Make a few mistakes and you could become a one-bite snack for a T-Rex.

Before you warm up your time machine, consider what you need to know:

(1) Where do you go to find dinosaurs? What are the best locations?

(2) When were the dinosaurs there? You want to arrive at a time when there will be dinosaurs present. In addition, it probably would be a bad idea to pop into existence at a location that was under water at the time you arrive. Dinosaurs do not live underwater, and unless you are using a submarine for a time machine, you cannot survive underwater either.

(3) You also need the same skills used today to find animals in the wild. The most important is the ability to identify and track the dinosaur based on the footprints it leaves behind.

Animal tracks, including dinosaur tracks reveal important information about the animal. For example, knowing where it is going and how fast it is moving, is important. However, you need to

Introduction

know more than that.

> "I was learning to track rhinoceroses in Africa and tracked right up on an animal that really I thought was going to kill me." — Martha Beck

It is the same today. If you want to photograph a rhinoceros, or bear, or a dinosaur, you need to be able to read the signs they leave. Dinosaur tracks can reveal how big the dinosaur is, what type of dinosaur it is, and how fast it is moving. Important information, if you want to survive and return with your photos.

So let us get started. We will learn about dinosaur tracks by studying fossilized dinosaur footprints. Then we will figure out how far back in time you need to go to safely find large numbers of living dinosaurs. ENJOY! Even if you do not own a time machine, you will learn a lot about dinosaurs and the history of our world.

Beginner's Guide To Tracking Dinosaurs

Introduction

Then God said, "Let Us make man in Our image, according to Our likeness; and let them rule over the fish of the sea and over the birds of the sky and over the cattle and over all the earth, and over every creeping thing that creeps on the earth." God created man in His own image, in the image of God He created him; male and female He created them.

～ Genesis 1:26-27

Beginner's Guide To Tracking Dinosaurs

CHAPTER 1
TYPES OF DINOSAURS

We will be learning how to track dinosaurs. However, before getting started it will be useful to know a little about dinosaurs. When you start tracking one, it will be handy to know what you are tracking.

To begin there are a few special words that are useful to know. These are words commonly used when talking about dinosaur tracks. Don't worry. They may seem strange at first, but they are easy words. Here they are:

Theropod – a type of three-toed carnivore (meat eater) dinosaur. T-Rex and raptors are theropods.

Ornithopod – another type of three-toed dinosaur, this time a herbivore (plant eater). Ornithopods leave footprints similar to those of a theropod.

Grallator – a type of small theropod dinosaur footprint.

Eubrontes - a type of large theropod dinosaur footprint.

Trackway - a trail of footprints made by a single dinosaur.

There are more words to learn and we will pick them up as we go along. By the end of chapter eight, you will know more about dinosaur tracks than 99.9% of all people and be in a good position

Types of Dinosaurs

to track dinosaurs.

Pubis Bones Are the Difference

Dinosaurs are divided into two categories: Saurischia (lizard-hipped) and Ornithischia (bird-hipped). What distinguishes one from the other is the orientation of their pubis bone (see figure 1). In Ornithischia dinosaurs, it points toward the back of the dinosaur and in Saurischia dinosaurs, this bone points forward. Why are dinosaurs categorized based on their pubis bone? Because in 1888 British paleontologist Harry Govier Seeley noticed a similarity between dinosaur hips and the hips of other animals and used that similarity to divide dinosaurs into two categories.

The Saurischia dinosaurs include theropods such as T-Rex and raptors. Theropod footprints are the most common type of dinosaur footprints, so we will be seeing a lot of those. Theropods are carnivorous and they walk on two legs.

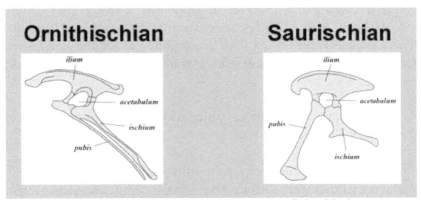

Figure 1: The two types of dinosaurs are distinguished by differences in the pubis bone.

Although they physically look very different but both T-Rex, a carnivore, and the huge long-necked plant-eating dinosaurs such as Supersaurus, are categorized as Saurischia.

Everyone either loves T-Rex, or is afraid of T-Rex. It is the most popular dinosaur. However, T-Rex did not leave many fossil footprints. Most of the fossil tracks we will be looking at are the three toed type thought to have been made by carnivorous dinosaurs classified as Coelurosauria. Both T-Rex and the Ceolosaurs are theropod dinosaurs.

Ornithischia dinosaurs are mainly herbivores and include the ornithopod dinosaurs that most likely made the other type of fossil footprint we will be examining. In addition to ornithopods, this category includes other well-known dinosaurs such as Triceratops and the Stegosaurs.

Figure 2: The dinosaur in the foreground is a Coelophysis. The larger one in the background is a Dilophosaurus.

Theropod Dinosaur Tracks

Most of the dinosaur tracks we will be looking at are theropod footprints. In the above image, there are two theropods. The smaller dinosaur in the foreground is a Coelophysis. Some experts say that a similar dinosaur made the smaller three-toed tracks, known as Grallator tracks that you will see in many of our examples.

The larger dinosaur is a Dilophosaurus. The experts at Dinosaur State Park (Rocky Hill, CT) have proposed this as the dinosaur that made the larger tracks we will be looking at,[1] called Eubrontes tracks. On the other hand, other experts say all of the theropod tracks we will be examining were made by the same type of dinosaur, just different sizes, juvenile, young adult, and adult. So, there are some disagreements. The bottom line is that no one knows for sure which theropod dinosaur made which tracks. The best we can say is that certain

---

[1] Most of the tracks you will see in this book are in our museum in Oregon.

Types of Dinosaurs

three-toed tracks were made by a theropod dinosaur. This is why fossil dinosaur tracks are not named for the dinosaur that made them. With living animals, tracks have the name of the animal that made them… bear tracks, moose tracks, cougar tracks, etc. We see the living animal and can observe the tracks it leaves. Dinosaur are no longer around, and their fossils are not found with the tracks they made.[2] That means we cannot know for sure which specific dinosaur made which tracks. This is why fossil dinosaur tracks are given separate names, Grallator and Eubrontes for example, based on their size and characteristics

> **Key Fact:**
>
> Fossil dinosaur footprints are not named for the dinosaur that made them. Fossil footprints are named based on their size and characteristics. The dinosaur that made a footprint typically cannot be positively identified.

Ornithopod Dinosaur Tracks

A bipedal, herbivorous ornithopod dinosaur made the other type of fossil track we will be looking at. However, there is no agreement on what type of ornithopod. Some say it may have been a Scutellosaurus. However, Scutellosaurus does not seem to have been large enough to have made some of the larger tracks. We are going to go with just a generic ornithopod without trying to be specific about which dinosaur made the tracks.

Sauropod (Long Neck) Dinosaurs

Because of their huge size, the long-neck Sauropods are easily recognized. We do not have Sauropod footprints in our museum.

---

[2] It is interesting to note that dinosaur tracks are frequently found in sediment layers that are significantly lower (older) than the sediment layers where the bone fossils of the dinosaur, thought to have made the tracks, are found.

Beginner's Guide To Tracking Dinosaurs

They are difficult to come by and not very interesting to look at. They often simply look like a round hole in the ground. In many cases, a trackway is needed for the impressions to be identified as sauropod footprints.

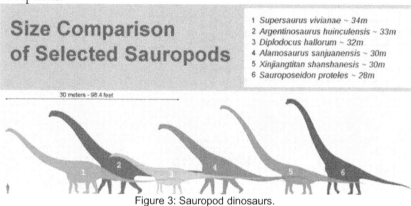
Figure 3: Sauropod dinosaurs.

Sauropod Tracks

Below is a photograph of sauropod footprints in the Paluxy River in Dinosaur Valley State Park in Texas. As you can see, they look like a circular hole in the ground. The larger hole (foot print) was made by a rear foot and the smaller hole is a front foot. The photo in the upper left corner shows part of an exhibit in the park's museum showing sauropod foot bones mounted in a sauropod footprint.

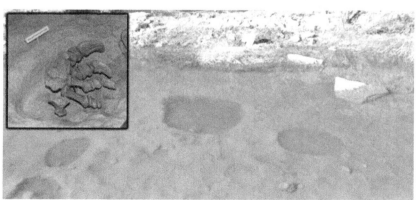
Figure 4 – Sauropod dinosaur tracks in the Paluxy River. The inset in the upper left corner shows the bone structure of a Sauropod foot.

Types of Dinosaurs

Figure 5 – Sauropod footprints often look like old post holes. A trackway, such as this one in the Purgatoire track site in Colorado, makes it easier to identify these holes as Sauropod tracks.

CHAPTER 2
HOW TRACKS ARE MADE

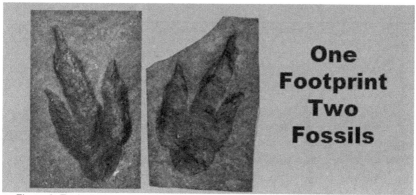

Figure 6: Each dinosaur footprint makes two fossil tracks. An impressed track and a natural cast called a raised track.

How were fossil dinosaur tracks made?

The answer is obvious. We do it whenever we step in mud or wet sand. The dinosaur steps in mud and leaves behind a footprint. However, in the dinosaur's case that footprint became a fossil... actually, each footprint often becomes two fossil tracks. Both result from the one footprint. That is what you see in the above photo. Both of those fossil dinosaur tracks came from the same footprint. Notice how they are mirror images.

Here is what happens: The dinosaur steps in the wet sediment and leaves a footprint. A new layer of sediment is deposited, filling

How Tracks Are Made

in and covering the footprint. The sediment turns to stone. When the rock is cracked open (see Appendix B), the bottom portion has the depression made by the dinosaur's foot. The top is a natural cast, a raised impression of the footprint. Both are considered original fossil footprints.

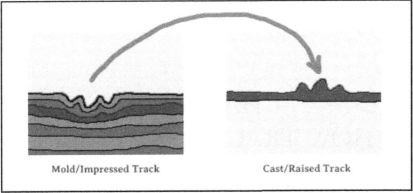

Figure 7 – The dinosaur steps in wet sediment leaving an impression of its foot. Another layer of sediment covers the footprint. When that layer is split off, the result is two fossil footprints. An impressed track and a raised track.

Impressed / Raised Tracks

The above image is a sketch showing the two tracks, with the upper raised track lifted off and set to the side. There you have it. Two fossil dinosaur tracks from a single footprint.

Sounds simple, but real-life is more complicated. In this example, the rock split exactly where the dinosaur's foot stepped in the soft sediment. This is known as a true print, or true track. When looking at fossil dinosaur footprints, a true track can be identified because it will have more detail than an underprint. For example, footpads and skin impressions may be visible on a true track.

However, the rock does not always split where we would like it to split. First, there is no way to see inside the rock. Before a rock is split no one knows if there is a dinosaur track or where the rock needs to be split to reveal the track. Secondarily, there are few options for where the rock will split. The rock will only split at a weak point, such as where there is mica or a biofilm.

Beginner's Guide To Tracking Dinosaurs

The Rock Splits Where There Is Mica

The tracks in our museum are in a sedimentary rock known as shale. In this case the shale will spilt where there is mica. The rock will not split anywhere else. If there is no mica, what you will have is a solid rock.

Notice in figure 7 the layers of sediment beneath the footprint are bent, taking on a less distinct impression of the footprint. The footprint impression goes deeper than the layer of sediment the dinosaur's foot touched.

Dinosaur Tracks – Underprints

If the mica layer is below the layer the dinosaur's foot touched, the rock will split at that lower location. This reveals a less distinct impression of the footprint called an underprint.

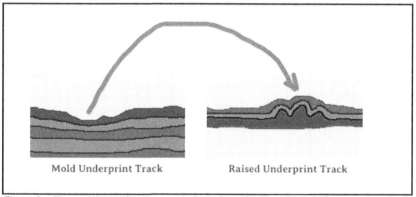

Figure 8 – The rock has split at a point below where the dinosaur's foot touched the sediment. This results in a less distinct underprint. Both the impressed track and the raised track are underprints.

Figure 8 shows the same rock as figure 7, but this time it split at a lower sediment layer revealing an underprint. Underprints have less detail than a true print. While a true print may clearly show footpads and skin impressions, underprints do not have much detail. At times, they may retain the impressions of all three toes and the claws, but in other instances, the underprint may be barely recognizable as a dinosaur footprint. However, it is still a real dinosaur fossil footprint.

How Tracks Are Made

Overprints

An overprint is similar to an underprint. An overprint is produced when the rock splits at a location above the sediment layer the dinosaur's foot touched. The result is a less distinct foot impression. If you have an individual track that does not show details, it may be either an under or overprint.

Sediment Quality

Another factor that effects the quality of the footprint is the consistency and quality of the wet sediment. A hard, nearly dry sediment layer can result in shallow impressions that may still have a lot of detail. Soft sediment will result in deep impressions with little detail. Soft sediment may also result in parts of the track collapsing and distorting the shape of the footprint.

And, of course, the weight of the dinosaur may impact track quality. A small dinosaur may not leave tracks. A large dinosaur, walking on the same sediment, may leave deep footprint impressions.

Sound confusing? Don't worry. By the end of chapter eight, you will be able to track a dinosaur.

CHAPTER 3
HOW ARE DINOSAUR TRACKS NAMED?

Dinosaurs rarely died in their footprints, so we can never be sure which specific dinosaur made a certain footprint. This means there is one naming system for dinosaurs and a separate naming system for their fossilized dinosaur tracks.

> "It is worth noting however, that the practice of naming an animal on the basis of a track is essentially an existential operation. Short of finding a skeleton of a diagnosable animal in a trackway, we can never be certain of the trackmaker. Even if we had such an occurrence, how could we establish that other species might not have made identical tracks? This is one of the main reasons for the separation of ichnotaxonomic nomenclature from biological taxonomy. Current procedure dictates that the track be named, not the unknowable animal that made it."[3]

Our tracks come from the Nash Dinosaur Track Quarry in the Connecticut River Valley in Massachusetts, an area with an abundance of dinosaur tracks (see Appendix B). Seven different types of tracks have been identified in about an 80 mile stretch of the valley,

---

[3] Olsen, Smith, and McDonald, "Type Material of the Type Species of the Classic Theropod Footprint" 1998, Society of Vertebrate Paleontology

How Are Dinosaur Tracks Named?

with several other rare types of tracks remaining unidentified. Let's start by looking at the theropod tracks.

The Most Common Dinosaur Track: Theropod Tracks

Three variations of theropod tracks have been named. It was originally thought these tracks were made by three different dinosaurs. However, many experts now believe they were made by the same type of dinosaur at different stages of growth: juvenile, young adult and full adult. For example,

> "It is probable that Anchisauripus tracks—15 to 25 centimeters (6 to 10 inches) long—are the footprints of large individuals of the Grallator trackmaker."[4]

In addition, it has been noted that:

> "It is very hard to distinguish these three ichnogenera [types of footprints] from one another because they constitute a graded series in which shape changes with size."[5]

In other words, the experts are not sure what dinosaur made which track, or if the same type of dinosaur made all of them, and in any case it is difficult to distinguish one type of theropod track from another. However, the naming nomenclature remains in use, so that is what we will use. The three types of theropod tracks are primarily identified by size as measured from the tip of the claw on the center toe to the back of the heel. They are:

Grallator: 3 to 6 inches;

Anchisauripus: 6 to 10 inches,

Eubrontes: 10 to 20 inches.

---

[4] David B. Weishampel and Luther Young, "Dinosaurs of the East Coast," John Hopkins University Press, (1996), page 98

[5] LeTourneau, McDonald, Olsen, Ku and Getty, "Fossils and Facies of the Connecticut Valley Lowland," page B2-19

Beginner's Guide To Tracking Dinosaurs

.It is estimated that several billion[6] dinosaur tracks have been found. They are found on every continent, except Antarctica. These three types of theropod tracks are, by far, the most common types of dinosaur tracks found around the world

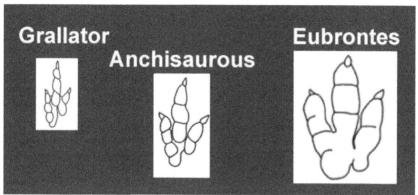

Figure 9 - The three types of theropod tracks are primary distinguished by size.

Two Questionable Fossil Footprints

Gigandipus tracks are 10 to 20 inches and are rarely found. They are thought to have been made by a theropod dinosaur similar to a Dilophosaurus. They are distinguished from other tracks by two characteristics: tail dragging and the presence of a hallux toe

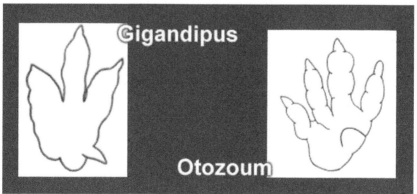

Figure 10 – Two rare types of Connecticut Valley dinosaur tracks.

---

[6] Martin Lockley, "Tracking Dinosaurs," Cambridge University Press, (1991), first page inside the cover (not numbered)

How Are Dinosaur Tracks Named?

(dew claw). All dinosaurs have a hallux toe, but it normally does not leave an impression in the ground. As seen in figure 10, the hallux is the small toe on the right side of the heel.

Gigandipus tracks look very much like Eubrontes tracks. For this reason, some scientists believe they were made by the same dinosaur as the maker of Eubrontes tracks, but walking with a different stance, or in different conditions.

Otozoum tracks are rare. They were made by what is thought to be a large, bipedal, dinosaur, possibly similar to a Plateosaurus. However, no one knows for sure what type of dinosaur made these tracks. The shape and structure of the foot does not match any known dinosaur.[7]

Anomoepus and Batrachopus

Both of the illustrations below show two footprints. These are animals that walked on four legs. The larger print is from the rear foot (pes). The small impression is that of a front foot (manus)

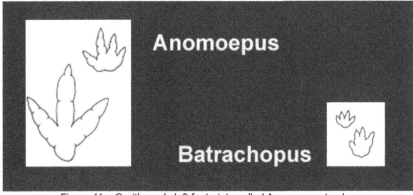

Figure 11 – Ornithopods left footprints called Anomoepus tracks. Batrachopus tracks are fairly common and are thought to have been made by a small crocodile-like animal.

Anomoepus tracks are typically 3 to 6 inches in size. They were made by an Ornithischian dinosaur (herbivore). The dinosaur that

---

[7] It is assumed that these tracks were made by a dinosaur because, based on the evolutionary timeline, dinosaurs were supposedly the only large animals living at the time these tracks were made. However, if all of these tracks are the result of a global flood (Noah's flood), Otozoum tracks may have been made by a large non-dinosaur animal.

made these tracks was usually bi-pedal, but at times, it walked on all fours. Anomoepus tracks are the second type of track we will be looking at in more detail.

Batrachopus tracks are not dinosaur tracks. They were made by what is thought to be a small crocodilian-like reptile. Batrachopus tracks are typically one inch or smaller. I am mentioning them because they are common and sometimes found on the same stone as a dinosaur track.

Sauropods and Triceratops Tracks

What about tracks made by other types of dinosaurs.?

Three-toed theropod tracks are, by far, the most common fossil dinosaur track. Sauropod tracks are also fairly common. However, being somewhat like a posthole, they are not as informative nor as interesting as the three-toed tracks.

Tracks made by other types of dinosaurs, such as Triceratops (ceratopsians) and Stegosaurs are virtually non-existent. Dinosaur track experts Martin Lockley and Adrian Hunt explain:

> "The rarity of ceratopsian tracks, prior to the discovery in the Laramie Formation, flamed a debate about the scarcity of certain track types. The debate turned on the puzzle that the tracks of most large quadrupedal ornithischian dinosaurs—especially ceratopsians, ankylosaurs, and stegosaurs—are rare or unknown, whereas their skeletal remains are common, even abundant in places. This puzzle is all the more intriguing when one considers that the rarity of these tracks cannot be attributed to a trackmaker being so small that it fails to depress the sediments; these particular trackmakers were heavy animals. At present there are still no well-accepted examples of stegosaur tracks and only a few convincing examples of ankylosaur tracks. Few ceratopsian tracks are known from deposits other than the Laramie Formation. How can this track sparsity be explained?"[8]

That final sentence presents an interesting question. Based on the limitations of evolutionary thinking, finding the answer is difficult. Lockley and Hunt speculate:

---

[8] Martin Lockley and Adrian Hunt, "Dinosaur Tracks and other Fossil Footprints of the Western United States," Columbia University Press, 1995, pages 229 & 231

How Are Dinosaur Tracks Named?

> "One appealing argument for the scarcity of large, quadrupedal tracks of the ornithischian group of dinosaurs is that the trackmakers generally, or frequently, avoided wet habitats or environments where tracks are most often preserved."[9]

However, they go on to point out this is not likely. The ceratopsian tracks found in the Laramie Formation were made in the same wet sediment as a large number of three-toed tracks. There are also a variety of non-dinosaur tracks in this same sediment. They thus turn to saying these types of tracks are scarce…

> "because paleontologists have not looked enough for rare tracks, or they have failed to look in the right places."[10]

On the other hand, there is another possibility. Michael Oard writes:

> "Since all dinosaur tracks are associated with water—either because of the sedimentary environment or because of the burial of tracks—it is worth assessing the swimming ability of various dinosaurs… Several types were probably poor swimmers. These would include the stegosaurs, with their tall plates and spiked tail; the ceratopsians, with their thick head plate and spikes; and the ankylosaurs, with their bulky bodies and spike."[11]

Facing the rising waters from a global flood, a good question to ask is, "How long can a dinosaur tread water?" The answer, for some dinosaurs, may have been, "Not very long."

---

[9] Ibid

[10] Ibid

[11] Michael J. Ord, "Dinosaur Challenges and Mysteries," Creation Book Publishers, (2011), page 93

CHAPTER 4
THEROPOD DINOSAUR TRACKS

Billions of dinosaur tracks have been found around the world. The most common tracks, by far, are the three-toed theropod tracks similar to the one shown here.

Figure 12 – Theropod dinosaur track

For those of you who plan to go back in time and photograph dinosaurs, you need to know what type of dinosaur made the tracks you are following. A large theropod could make a quick meal of you. On the other hand, an ornithopod dinosaur, a herbivore, might be safer to photograph. Theropods and ornithopods leave different, but

Theropod Dinosaur Tracks

similar three-toed tracks. You can tell which is which, if you know what to look for.

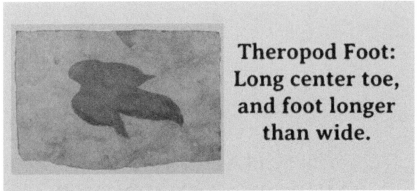

Figure 13 – theropod footprints are longer than they are wide.

Theropod: Long Center Toe

The first thing you may have noticed in figures 12 and 13 are the center toes. Theropod footprint impressions often have a center toe that is significantly longer than the toes on either side.

Second, notice the toes on either side are close in to the foot. The foot impression is noticeably longer than wide.

It is important to keep in mind that dinosaur footprints were made by a living animal in a medium (mud) that can vary greatly. That means foot impressions can vary greatly, and that means some theropod footprints will not have all of these characteristics. What we look for is an identification supported by a preponderance of the evidence.

Theropod: Side Toe and Claws

Another characteristics of a theropod footprint is that the inside toe appears to be attached to the side of the foot, while the outside toe goes all of the way back to the heel.

A fourth characteristic is that theropods have larger and more distinct claws. Ornithopods (herbivores) typically leave small triangular shaped claw impressions. For both types of dinosaurs, the claws tend to make the deepest impression. When the footprint is faint,

Beginner's Guide To Tracking Dinosaurs

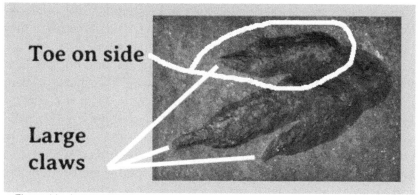

Figure 14 – Large, sharp claws and a toe that appears to be attached on the side are characteristics of a theropod dinosaur footprint.

the claw impressions often will be the easiest part of the footprint to spot. When examining rocks to find dinosaur footprints, begin by looking for claw impressions.

Theropods are Living Animals

These are the four key characteristics that distinguish a theropod footprint (carnivore) from an ornithopod footprint (herbivore).

(1) Long center toe
(2) The foot is longer than it is wide
(3) Large claws
(4) One toe appears to be attached to the side of the foot

These are not hard and fast rules. Dinosaurs are living animals. They will move their feet in different ways as they walk, or even when standing still. Therefore, each footprint can be slightly different. In addition, mud is a dynamic medium that takes on impressions in different ways depending on the characteristics of the mud. At times theropod footprints do not have all four, or even any of these characteristics. A trackway may start out looking like theropod tracks, and then suddenly several tracks later they look like ornithopod tracks. Did the dinosaur suddenly morph into a different dinosaur? No. The way the foot was placed changed, or the character of the mud changed. Possibly the footprint was distorted by another animal. Or a combination of these or something else. However, when all four characteristics are clearly present you can be confident you are looking at a theropod footprint. When few characteristics are seen, it may be difficult to positively identify the type of dinosaur.

Here is an important lesson. Information about dinosaurs (and fossils in general) is often presented in a manner that makes it seem the experts know all the answers. They do not. When it comes to fossils, there is a lot of guesswork and many assumptions. It may be that these are sincere guesses and the assumptions are made with good intentions, but that does not make them correct. We need to look at all the facts, understand when assumptions are being made, and logically discern when we are dealing with factual conclusions, and when we are dealing with conclusions based on guesses and assumptions.

We also need to keep in mind we are dealing with historical science, not empirical science. Empirical science uses observations, repeatable experiments and calibrated measurements to produce facts. However, we cannot observe, nor do experiments, nor directly measure things in the past. For example, we cannot observe a dinosaur walking and leaving footprints. Therefore, when there is no record of direct observations.[12] Historical science uses a preponderance of the evidence to arrive at a conclusion.

---

[12] Courtroom trials use the techniques of historical science. Just like in a trial, an eyewitness provides the most compelling testimony about the past. We do have written eyewitness documentation recording observations of dinosaurs (but not dinosaur tracks). We will get to one of those in the chapter on eating dinosaurs (chapter 10, page 49).

CHAPTER 5
ORNITHOPOD DINOSAUR TRACKS

In the same location where our theropod dinosaur tracks are found, there are also some ornithopod tracks, but they are rare. There are differences of opinion concerning the type of dinosaur, that made the ornithopod racks. Some experts say it was a dinosaur similar to Scutellosaurus. Others are not so sure. Most experts simply say they are unable to identify the specific type of ornithopod. In any case, it is all guesswork until someone finds a dinosaur that died in its tracks. For our study we will go with a generic ornithopod designation.

The name "ornithopod" means "bird foot." Like the theropods, ornithopods leave three-toed tracks. Birds also leave tracks with three forward facing toes, and so the name "bird foot" for these dinosaurs.

Most ornithopods have a two-legged, bipedal stance, although they will sometimes walk using all four limbs, leaving both front and back foot impressions.

As with theropod tracks, ornithopod fossil footprints can either be impressed or raised. However that can be difficult to see in a photograph. Fortunately, whether it is impressed or raised is not critically important when learning about track characteristics.

The image on the next page shows an impressed ornithopod fossil footprint. As with most of the tracks in this book, the track has been stained at the quarry to make it easier to see the impression.

Ornithopod Dinosaur Tracks

Ornithopod, More of a Square

Notice that the track is close to being as wide as it is long, much more so than the theropod footprint. The toes on either side are spread wider. In addition, the center toe is typically shorter than a theropod center toe, when compared with the side toes.

Figure 15 – An ornithopod dinosaur footprint

I know I have said this before, but it is important. Keep in mind that with fossil footprints we are looking at impressions made by a living animal in a muddy sediment that is highly variable. That means there is a huge variability in tracks. For example, an ornithopod may drag the tip of its center toe as it steps forward. This extends the center toe impression, making it appear longer. On the other hand, some tracks made by an ornithopod dinosaur may not have all of the characteristics of a typical ornithopod dinosaur footprint. To make a positive identification of a footprint outside of a trackway, we need to find multiple identifying characteristics.

Equal Side Toes and Small Claws

Three other characteristics that help distinguish an ornithopod track from a theropod track are that the claws are smaller and triangular shaped; the angle of the toes on either side of the foot is about the same for each toe, such that both toes angle toward the heel; and the heel is wider and rounder than on a theropod's foot.

Beginner's Guide To Tracking Dinosaurs

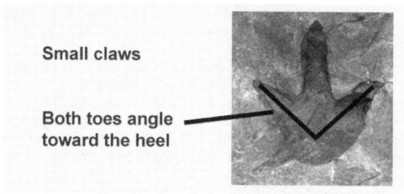

Figure 16 – Characteristics of an ornithopod footprint.

Did you notice that this fossil has an impression not normally seen on dinosaur tracks. What is that pointing from the foot toward the lower left corner of stone (figure 16)? What you are seeing is the "dew claw," also known as a hallux toe. Both theropod and ornithopod dinosaurs have this toe, but it typically does not leave an impression. Because dinosaurs walk on their toes, as with a dog, the hallux toe rarely contacts the ground.

Ornithopod vs Theropod Footprints

In figure 17 you see theropod and ornithopod footprints side-by-side. If you were tracking a dinosaur in the wild, you should now be able to identify which track belongs to a meat eater and which belongs to a vegetarian.

Figure 17 – A theropod footprint on the left and ornithopod footprint on the right.

Ornithopod Dinosaur Tracks

Summary of the Differences

The ornithopod footprint is wider; the heel is rounder; the side toes are about equal in size; and the claws are smaller.

For theropods the claws are larger and more distinct; the overall footprint is long and narrow; the center toe is longer in comparison with the side toes; and one of the side toes appears to go all of the way back to the heel while the other appears to be attached on the side of the foot

If you a tracking a dinosaur, it is important to know whether it is a carnivore or herbivore. You now know how to tell the difference. However, do not run out and start tracking down a dinosaur just yet. There is more you need to know. For example, how big is it? We will answer that question, but first, a very short chapter describing how dinosaur toes are numbered.

CHAPTER 6
NUMBERING DINOSAUR TOES

It may sound a little strange, but animal toes, including dinosaur toes, are numbered. This provides an easy and accurate way to refer to a specific toe such that everyone knows which toe is being discussed.

Our collection of dinosaur track fossils mainly consists of theropod and ornithopod footprints. These are three-toed footprints made by dinosaurs that walk on their toes. This is not uncommon. Dogs and cats walk on their toes. It is called digitgrade walking. Digitgrade animals generally move quicker than those that put their feet flat on the ground (plantigrade).

Humans are plantigrade, meaning we walk with our ankle bones near the ground. In addition, we are unique in being the only ones who land on our heels when we are running[13].

Although both theropod and ornithopod dinosaurs commonly leave three-toed footprints, they actually have four toes. There is a hallux toe, called a dew claw on dogs, that normally does not touch the ground. The hallux toe is on the inside of the foot and is numbered as toe #1. (Note that numbering of toes is traditionally done using Roman Numerals.)

We then go around the foot numbering the toes in order. The next toe is number "II" (#2). What is commonly seen as the center

---

[13] https://breakingmuscle.com/fitness/the-mechanics-of-human-running

Numbering Dinosaur Toes

toe is number "III" (#3). The toe on the outside of the foot is number "IV" (#4).

Let's look at the bones in a dinosaur's foot to see how this works. Figure 18 shows the numbering of the toes on the right foot of a theropod dinosaur. We know this is a right foot because the hallux toe is always on the inside of the foot.

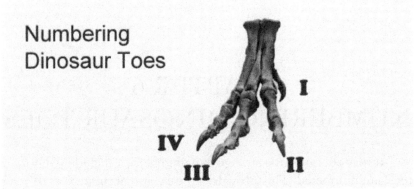

Figure 18 – Toes are numbered using Roman numerals. The hallux toe (#I) normally does not leave an impression.

Looking at a fossil theropod dinosaur footprint (below) we can see how this numbering works.

The #I toe (hallux) did not leave an impression. On theropods the toe that appears to be attached to the side of the foot is on the inside of the foot. Since there is no #I toe impression, we start numbering the toes with #II.

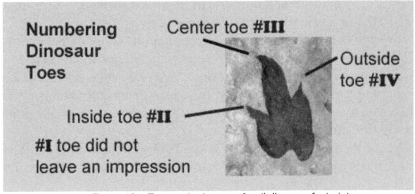

Figure 19 – Toe numbering on a fossil dinosaur footprint.

CHAPTER 7
READING DINOSAUR TRACKS

The size and shape of a theropod dinosaur footprint gives us additional information about the dinosaur.

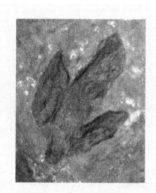 

Figure 20 – What can you learn from these footprints?

Look at the footprint on the left in figure 20. This is an impressed track (indented into the rock). Notice that the toe on the left side appears to be attached to the side of the foot. That is one characteristic indicating a theropod made this footprint. In addition, the toe that appears to be on the side of the foot is always on the inside of the foot. That means the dinosaur's right foot made this footprint.

Next look at the tip of the center toe. Notice that it bends slightly to the left. For theropods the tip of the center toe tends to

What Else Can You Learn From A Dinosaur Track?

bend toward the inside of the foot. That is another indication this is a right foot.

Take a look at the footprint on the right (figure 20). Is this a left or right foot? The tip of the center toe is not noticeably bent, but the toe on the right appears to be slightly closer to the heel than the toe on the left. That would indicate this may be a right foot. Yes, this track is harder to read. Dinosaur tracks were made by living animals. They could flex their toes and move them independently. They could change their stance. In addition, the footprint was made in a medium (mud) that varies greatly. That means dinosaur tracks are highly variable and their identification may not always be clear. It also means this track, which most likely is a theropod right foot, may not be a right foot or even a theropod footprint.[14] Not every footprint is a good source of information about the dinosaur. When you are tracking a dinosaur, do not jump to conclusions.

Here is something interesting to do if you visit a museum that has a dinosaur on display with footprints. Check to see if the footprints are correct for the left and right feet. Museums usually have good quality footprints, but sometimes they do not pay attention to which foot goes where. At times they are not even the correct footprints for the type of dinosaur.

Looking At Raised Tracks

In a photograph it can be difficult to know if you are looking at a raised or impressed footprint. Figure 21 shows a raised track. When you are looking at raised tracks you need to keep in mind that it is a mirror image.

Notice the track has large claws. The center toe is long, and the footprint is longer than it is wide. One toe (the one on the bottom of the image) appears to be attached to the side of the foot. It is a theropod footprint. However, is it a right or left foot?

---

[14] This is most likely a theropod footprint. This track is definitely longer than it is wide. And it has a more pointed heel compared with the rounded heel of an ornithopod.

Beginner's Guide To Tracking Dinosaurs

Figure 21 – Theropod right foot, raised natural cast

A raised track is a natural cast of the dinosaur's footprint. When a rock is split, the raised foot impression is on the bottom side of the section of rock that was split off. To see that impression we needed to turn the rock over. That means what we are seeing is a footprint for which the right and left sides are swapped. Look at the back of your left hand. Your thumb is on the right. Now turn your hand over and look at the palm of your hand. Your thumb is now on the left. That is what we are seeing when we look at a raised track. It is a mirror image of an impressed footprint.

Notice the tip of the center toe and claw bends slightly downward in this photo. In addition, the toe that appears to be attached to the side of the foot is on the bottom of the picture. That means this is a right foot. Do you see it? Remember you are looking at a reversed image (mirror image).

Although this foot impression is very high quality, we have made this one more difficult to see by looking at a raised track turned on its side. However, you have seen this track before (page 23), and all the characteristics of a theropod's right foot are there.

How Big Was This Dinosaur?

To get the approximate size of the dinosaur, measure the footprint from the tip of the center toe claw, to the back of the heel. For this track, that is about six inches. This is the dinosaur's foot length.

What Else Can You Learn From A Dinosaur Track?

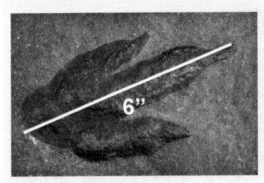

Figure 22 – The length of the foot provides an estimate of the size

To get the height of the dinosaur at its hip, multiply the foot length by four. In this example, that gives us 24 inches. The dinosaur that made this footprint stood about two feet high at the hip. Please note, this is a rough estimate. The ratio varies from four (used here) to five. It would be equally valid to multiply the six inch foot length by five to get a hip height of 30 inches. That is a variation of six inches, but it is as close as we can get.

To get the size of the dinosaur take the number of inches in the foot size and multiply it by 12. That gives the length of the dinosaur from the tip of its nose to the tip of its tail. In our example, the foot length is six inches. That means the dinosaur is 72 inches (six feet) from its nose to the end of its tail. Again, this is a rough estimate. Some, instead of multiplying by 12, will multiply by 10. Just like people, there is variation in dinosaurs. Some small people have proportionally large feet, and some large people have proportionally smaller feet. What we can say is this dinosaur was probably between five and six feet from nose to tail.

Remember, these formulas only give an approximation. The ratio varies with the dinosaur. However, the above ratios do provide a reasonable estimate of the size of the dinosaur.

Beginner's Guide To Tracking Dinosaurs

How Fast Was The Dinosaur Going?

The ichnological record indicates that the vast majority of dinosaurs whose tracks were preserved were walking." – Lockley and Gillette[15]

The fossil record indicates that dinosaurs walked most of the time. However, that does not mean they could not run. Their cardio-vascular system appears to have been designed to support bursts of high energy activity, unlike birds that have a cardio-vascular system designed to support continuous high energy activity (flying). Imagine this situation... you were approaching a dinosaur, trying to get a selfie with the dinosaur in the background. You are downwind and moving quietly... until your foot breaks a small branch... the dinosaur turns toward you... do not assume the dinosaur will be slow moving. Do not try to outrun it. They can be fast. Freeze. Don't move and hopefully the dinosaur will not see you.

When tracking a dinosaur you can estimate how fast the dinosaur was moving. All that is needed is a series of three or more footprints (a trackway). Measuring them will give a rough estimate of the dinosaur's speed.

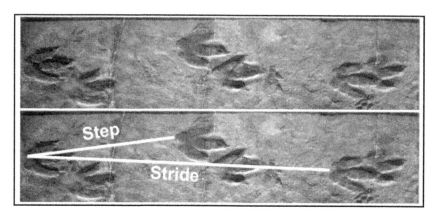

Figure 23 – Dinosaur speed can be estimated based on stride

---

[15] Published in "Dinosaur Tracks and Traces, Edited by David D. Gillette and Martin G., University of Cambridge Press (1989)

What Else Can You Learn From A Dinosaur Track?

Figure 23 shows two photographs of the same trackway,[16] the lower photograph has the step and stride marked. These photos show a double trackway. This is something you may encounter when tracking a dinosaur. Two different dinosaurs stepped in almost the same spots as their paths crossed. Look to see which set of footprints (trackway) is impressed into (is on top of) the other trackway.

Having at least three footprints allows us to measure both the step length (from the heel of a right foot to the heel of the next left foot step) and the stride length (from the heel of the right foot to the next impression of the heel of the right foot).

In the previous section we saw how to calculate the dinosaur's hip height based on the length of the foot. In that example the dinosaur had a hip height of 24 inches. To get the speed of the dinosaur divide the stride length (in inches) by the hip height (in inches).

If the resulting number is 1.0 or less, the dinosaur was walking.

If the resulting number is 1.0 up to 1.99, the dinosaur was trotting.

If the number is 2.0 or greater, the dinosaur was running.

Of course, these are just estimates, but they roughly show whether he dinosaur was taking its time, or was in a hurry. For the trackway in figure 23 the ratio is 1.5... this dinosaur was moving along. It was probably trotting.

---

[16] This is slab 45/1 in the Berneski Museum at Amherst College.

CHAPTER 8
CAN YOU SEE THE DINOSAUR TRACKS?

Now let's test your skills. Sometimes tracks are obvious and easy to see. Most often, they can be difficult to spot unless you know what to look for. A good place to start is to look for the claws. Claws tend to leave better impressions even when the toe and foot impressions are faint and difficult to see. Second, look for the general shape of a dinosaur track, and in particular the center toe.

Figure 24 – When you are looking at the ground, this may be what you see. Are there any dinosaur tracks on this stone?

There are five or more dinosaur tracks on the rock pictured above. Can you find any of them? Once you know what to look for

Can You See The Dinosaur Tracks?

it becomes easier to see tracks. However, trying to find tracks on a difficult stone such as this, and in a small black and white photograph in a book, can be difficult. I tried to make it as easy as possible. This photo was taken early in the morning when the sun was at just the right angle to highlight two of the larger tracks.[17]

This stone has some of the most difficult to spot dinosaur tracks in our collection. If you would like to give it a try with a higher resolution color image, the image is online at: www.AJ83.com/tracks

An image showing where one of the tracks is located can be seen at: www.AJ83.com/tracks-answer

Here are a couple of easier ones. Can you see a track or tracks on either of the stones pictured below? Can you identify the type of dinosaur?

Figure 25 – What do you see on these two stones?

The stone on the left has been stained to improve visibility. It looks like this was a mutant dinosaur with two center toes. This type of impression can happen in any of three ways. The dinosaur steps in the mud, then picks up a toe and moves it a little. Often this will be seen as the toe having multiple tips and claws. The dinosaur might also pick up its entire foot and then put it down in almost the same spot. The third possibility is that a second dinosaur stepped in an

---

[17] Finding tracks at high noon can be very difficult. The best time to look for tracks is in the early morning or late afternoon, when the sun is low on the horizon. This creates shadows that highlight the tracks.

existing footprint with the result being one footprint overlaying another footprint. I can assure you, dinosaurs did not have two center toes. BTW, did you recognize this as a theropod dinosaur track?

The stone on the right does not have any dinosaur tracks, but it does have an interesting fossil ripple. There was water flowing from the top of the photograph to the bottom. There was probably something stuck in the mud, possibly parts of a tree branch, and the water was flowing around them leaving two horseshoe shaped ripples in the sediment.[18]

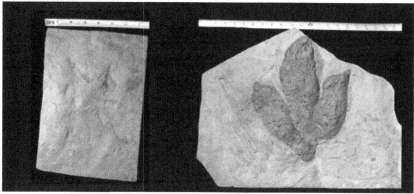

Figure 26 – The one on the right is obvious, but what do you see on the stone on the left?

In figure 26 the photo on the left is what you might see walking through an area thought to have dinosaur tracks. The track on this stone is in its natural condition (no highlighting). Start by looking for the claws. Do you see the large claw just above and to the right of the center of the stone? Now look to the left of that. You may be able to see a faint impression of another toe the almost goes all of the way to the bottom edge of the stone. There may be two tracks, one on top of the other. These are raised tracks that are most likely underprints. In is not uncommon for dinosaurs to leave incomplete prints such as these.

The track on the right has been stained making the track obvious. This is a Eubrontes track measuring about 14 inches from the

---

[18] For ripples such as this to fossilize requires very unique conditions. The water had to be heavily saturated with sediment, which settled out of moving water, doing so quickly so as to both create and bury the ripple. In other words, the ripples had to be buried in sediment as they were formed. There are no conditions existing today that could accomplish this.

Can You See The Dinosaur Tracks?

heel to the tip of the center toe. Also notice there are some straight impressions to the left of the track. They are difficult to see in the photograph, but they are there. These are fossilized wood impressions. The Nash Quarry, where this track came from, is unusual because there is a lot of fossil vegetation, mostly small pieces of wood. However, there is no sign of growing vegetation. The vegetation appears to have floated in from somewhere else. This is unusual, and thus noteworthy.

You now have the basics of tracking dinosaurs. A question that might come to mind is, why do billions of fossil dinosaur tracks exist, but we do not see such fossils forming today? What are the conditions that result in dinosaur footprints, or other animal tracks being preserved as fossils? Where, when, and why did those conditions exist in the past, and why do they not exist today? Answering these questions will help us pin down how far into the past you need to go to find dinosaurs.

CHAPTER 9
DINOSAUR TRACK MYSTERIES

If you are going to track down and photograph a dinosaur, how far back in time do you need to go?

Dinosaur tracks present us with a major mystery. The next time it rains go for a walk, and be sure to walk through some mud. You will leave footprints. Will those footprints be there next year? How about next month? What about next week? No. Do the same thing on a beach. You will leave footprints in the sand, but they will not last. Footprints in mud or sand are fragile. They quickly disappear. So why do we find billions of fossilized dinosaur footprints?

However, that is not the only mystery. The existence of dinosaur tracks raises many questions. For example,

Why are these billions of dinosaur tracks found on flat bedding planes, some of which extend over very large regions?[19] (A flat bedding plane is a flat layer of sediment. Sediment is always deposited in flat layers.)

Why is there rarely any evidence of vegetation (or food sources) where dinosaur tracks are found?

Why are many tracksites dominated by carnivorous theropod dinosaurs? Where are the herbivores? What were the carnivores eating?

---

[19] Martin Lockley, "Tracking Dinosaurs," Cambridge University Press, (1991) page 7

Dinosaur Track Mysteries

Dinosaur tracks are found in marine environments, something the experts say is impossible.[20]

Similar dinosaur tracks are found in multiple layers of sediment, one on top of the other, with some layers supposedly separated by millions of years.

> "When aspects of the tracks or trackways are similar across several layers of rock, it is difficult to accept that they were made by similar creatures in a similar environment that was preserved in a similar fashion, but all separated by millions of years."[21] – Michael Oard

Answering these questions, and others, will reveal much about the history of our world and help us nail down the time frame you should target with your time machine. Let's take on the biggest mystery, why were dinosaur tracks preserved?

Preserving Dinosaur Tracks

The most common theory is that dinosaurs stepped in mud along a lake shore leaving a footprint. The mud dried and hardened in the sun. The next annual flood brought more sediment which buried the hardened footprints. Then that new sediment layer eventually hardened.

> Patrolling daily for food, theropod dinosaurs left myriad tracks in shoreline muds and sands. Baked hard by exposure to the sun as lakes shrank further, the footprints were covered and preserved by fresh sediment introduced during wet intervals.[22]

We have those conditions today. There are rivers that annually flood, depositing new layers of sediment every year. There are lakes with fluctuating levels. Why do we not see animal tracks drying and baked hard by the sun today, resulting in fossils? Yet, there are billions

---

[20] https://answersingenesis.org/dinosaurs/footprints/fossilized-footprints-a-dinosaur-dilemma/

[21] Michael J. Ord, "Dinosaur Challenges and Mysteries," Creation Book Publishers, (2011), page 92

[22] LeTourneau; McDonald; Olsen; Ku; and Getty, "Fossils and Facies of the Connecticut Valley Lowland: Ecosystem Structure and Sedimentary Dynamics Along the Footwall Margin of an Active Rift" (2005), page 122

Beginner's Guide To Tracking Dinosaurs

of fossil dinosaur tracks. Something unique must have happened in the past that we do not see happening today.

Track Preservation Hypothesis.

The dinosaur tracks in our museum come from the Connecticut River Valley near Holyoke, Massachusetts (see appendix B). This is an area known for its abundance of dinosaur tracks. It has been assumed that during the time of the dinosaurs the area had a monsoonal climate. Part of the year had heavy rains, and the other part was arid and dry. This resulted in large lakes with annually fluctuating levels. As the water level dropped, the dinosaurs would have to walk along muddy shores to reach drinking water that continually was moving further away as the lake shrank during the dry season. The dinosaurs left footprints in the mud that baked in the sun, became hard, and were buried by sediment carried by the rising lake water during the next monsoon season.

However, There is a Problem

"Unlike the relatively robust bones of large animals, footprints can easily be destroyed by the first rain or wave that washes over them. They may also be obliterated by the next herd of animals that passes through the rea. The growth of vegetation may work its damage more slowly, but just as effectively. All in all, the likelihood that any single track or trackway will become a fossil is exceedingly small."[23] – Dinosaur track experts Martin Lockley and Adrian Hunt

"Studies of modern tracks reveal that footprints nevertheless deteriorate rapidly; they are usually destroyed within a few days or weeks."[24] – Dinosaur track experts Martin Lockley and Adrian Hunt

Mother Earth News gives advice on tracking present day animals in the wilderness. Here is what they say about the durability of animal tracks:

---

[23] Martin Lockley and Adrian Hunt, "Dinosaur tracks and Other Fossil Footprints of the Western United States," Columbia University Press, (1995), page 18

[24] Ibid

Dinosaur Track Mysteries

"Under most conditions, though, the peaks of a track — one made in, say, medium-hard garden soil — will have deteriorated or rounded somewhat after 24 hours. In another day, the mark may have accumulated debris, leaves, or pockmarks from raindrops. Eventually, as the track crumbles and fills or is covered by other prints, it will disappear completely."[25]

Animal tracks do not last long. Certainly not long enough to bake rock hard in the sun without some deterioration and collection of debris. At our museum, we have been examining cross sections of dinosaur tracks. Tracks are cut so that the layers of sediment within the track, along with anything that collected in the track, can be seen. We have never seen evidence of deterioration of the edges nor debris collection in a fossil dinosaur track. What is observed in the cross sections are thin layers of fine sediment showing a continuous process of sediment accumulation.

In addition, if the tracks were made during an annual wet season, and dried out and hardened during an annual dry season, there should be signs of vegetation. If a concrete sidewalk gets a small crack, something will soon be growing in that crack. Plants quickly take root. What we see with dinosaur tracks, and the surrounding sediment, are flat bedding planes with no signs of vegetation. No debris. No tiny roots. Just a flat landscape of mud.[26] That is very odd.

Preserving Dinosaur Footprints

Let us step back and answer a question that needs to be addressed before coming up with ideas for track preservation. What is required for dinosaur tracks to be preserved as fossils?

First, a dinosaur has to leave a footprint. That requires mud of a type and consistency that will retain the shape of the footprint. Step in the soft mud of a swamp or peat bog, and you will sink up to your knees and leave no footprint. Step in dry sand and you will leave a rounded depression that soon disappears with the wind.

It is interesting to note that in nearly every case individual dinosaur tracks are visible. Huh? Why is this interesting? If dinosaurs were

---

[25] https://tinyurl.com/y282skcx

[26] Typically, as water runs off a lakeshore, when the water level gets low it will produce some channeling. However, signs of channeling are rarely (if ever) seen in the flat sediment surfaces that have dinosaur tracks.

Beginner's Guide To Tracking Dinosaurs

repeatedly going to the shore of a lake to drink or feed on fish, they would walk on top of tracks that were made previously. The result would be what is called "dinoturbation." There are so many footprints that the ground is churned up and only the latest tracks may be visible within the churned up mud. Even mud that has hardened in the sun will break down when stepped on.

However, in most locations dinosaur tracks are individually discernable with no churning of the mud, or even significant overlapping. This is very odd. Either a very few dinosaurs infrequently came to the lake shore, or the tracks the dinosaurs made where quickly buried, at times even as they were being made. However, what could do that? The pieces of the puzzle are not coming together (yet).

Second, footprints, even in firm mud, are fragile. That means very soon after it was made the footprint must be protected by being buried. So rapid burial is required. However, since it is fragile, that burial must be gentle. An energetic burial will result in the footprint eroding. This is an unusual combination, rapid, but gentle burial.

Third, it must be buried deeply. A thin layer sediment offers no protection at all.

Expert Opinion Part II

The experts recognize the tracks hardening in the sun scenario is not realistic, so they are searching for alternatives. Here is the leading alternative:

> "There are, however, other explanations. One we favor pertains to the phenomenon of underprints… By their very nature, underprints are already buried at the time they were made. This means there is no problem explaining how they can be covered by the next layer of sediment without being eroded away… the surfaces remained wet most of the time and the animals, particularly large ones, sank in very deep, leaving underprints at depths less vulnerable to perturbation."[27]

As you can see, they are addressing the need for a quick, but gentle and deep burial. The problem is that the evidence does not support this hypothesis.

---

[27] Martin Lockley and Adrian Hunt, "Dinosaur tracks and Other Fossil Footprints of the Western United States," Columbia University Press, (1995), page 19

Dinosaur Track Mysteries

When quarrying dinosaur tracks, you cannot select where the rock will split, even if you could see inside the rock to know where the true track lies. The rock will split where there is mica or a biofilm. Most fossil tracks are underprints or overprints. So looking at the exposed rock surface does not necessarily help us answer the question.[28] However, many tracks are true tracks that have, for example, sharp claw, footpad, and even skin impressions. That level of detail does not happen with underprints.

In addition, what do we see if we look inside the rock? With the underprint hypothesis, we should see a solid mass of sediment filling in the foot impression above the true track. Based on this hypothesis, that type of infilling is needed to bury and preserve a true track.

Our museum is currently engaged in research in which we are looking at cross sections of dinosaur tracks. Figure 27 is a photograph of a typical cross section of a fossilized raised dinosaur toe impression. It shows the sediment layers that filled in the impressed dinosaur footprint. This raised track, if not at rue track, is very close to a true track. What we are seeing are the many fine layers of sediment that filled in the true track. There is no indication this fossil was formed as an underprint. What we see are multiple fine layers of sediment, that initially follow the contours of the foot impression, and gradually straighten, with some low energy accumulation. As we move higher, away from the true track, the layers straighten out to

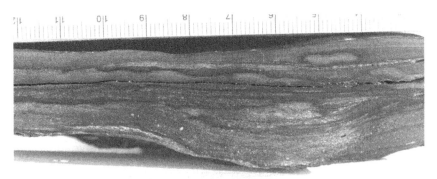

Figure 27 – cross section of a fossil toe showing the sediment layers within a raised dinosaur track.

---

[28] We are currently involved in a research project that is mapping fine sediment layers revealed on samples of shale containing multiple tracks. The early indications are that this study will provide additional supporting evidence concerning track formation and preservation by continuous sediment deposit..

Beginner's Guide To Tracking Dinosaurs

form a flat sediment surface. The indication is that filling of the track was a continuous process, with at least part of the infilling done by moving water, resulting in the low energy sediment capture.

An Even More Difficult Question

The photo below is a picture of the corner of a slab in the Berneski Museum at Amherst College. The entire slab is covered with fossil raindrop impressions. They look like small craters all over the surface of the rock. How is it possible for raindrop impressions to be preserved and fossilized? They do not make underprints. They are even more delicate than dinosaur footprints!

Figure 28 – Fossil raindrop impressions.

Try to imagine a situation in which raindrop impressions in mud would last long enough to become fossilized. No dinosaur walked on them. No animal walked on them. In addition, there are not many of them on this rock. It looks like a very brief shower blew through. Or perhaps they were very quickly submerged or buried, preventing additional raindrops from falling on this surface. If left exposed, even a little additional rain would create mud mush and wipe away the initial raindrop impressions. This fossil requires mud firm enough to take and hold the raindrop impression, and, it either was a very brief shower, or they were quickly, yet gently buried.

Raindrop fossils are not rare. You can buy rocks with raindrop impressions on EBay for prices as low as $25 to $30.

Dinosaur Track Mysteries

How could raindrop impression last long enough to become fossils?[29] That certainly is not happening today.

We are left with more questions than answers at this point, and the commonly proposed answers do not fit the observed evidence. However, as we continue we will get answers. Answers that are important for determining how far back in time you need to go to track down and photograph a dinosaur. By the way, since you will be going back to the days of the dinosaurs, have you considered having a dino burger while you are there?

---

[29] The slab pictured in part in figure 26 was collected in 1863 in Turner's Falls, Massachusetts. That is in the Connecticut River Valley about 33 miles north of where our dinosaur tracks were found. This rift valley that is open to the sea at its southern end. In addition, the patterns in, and composition of the sediment show that a large amount of sediment came in from the highlands east of the valley. It is easy to visualize parts of this valley, in particular the northern parts, being shielded from direct impact of the rising global floodwaters resulting from the early part of Noah's flood. There would be no direct impact from tsunamis, or even tides. So the rising and falling water levels would be much gentler, allowing dinosaur foot prints and even raindrop impressions to be preserved instead of washed away.

CHAPTER 10
ARE DINOSAURS GOOD TO EAT?

We have been using a hypothetical scenario of hunting dinosaurs with a camera. However, what if you needed to hunt a dinosaur for food? Would dinosaur meat be good to eat? There are no dinosaurs around today, but we do have a historical record that might help answer this question.

In the year 1271, a Venetian (Italian) merchant named Marco Polo traveled to China with his father and uncle. He stayed in China for 24 years serving as a tax collector for Kublai Khan and traveling throughout China. After returning to Europe, he published an account of his time in China called, *"The Travels of Marco Polo."* In that book he describes a creature that appears to be a dinosaur:

> "Here are seen huge serpents, ten paces in length, and ten spans in the girt of the body. At the fore part, near the head, they have two short legs, having three claws like those of a tiger, with eyes larger than a fourpenny loaf (pane da quattro denari) and very glaring. The jaws are wide enough to swallow a man, the teeth are large and sharp, and their whole appearance is so formidable, that neither man, nor any kind of animal, can approach them without terror.
>
> Others are met with of a smaller size, being eight, six, or five paces long; and the following method is used for taking them.

Are Dinosaurs Good To Eat?

In the daytime, by reason of the great heat, they lurk in caverns, from whence, at night, they issue to seek their food, and whatever beast they meet with and can lay hold of, whether tiger, wolf, or any other, they devour; after which they drag themselves towards some lake, spring of water, or river, in order to drink.

By their motion in this way along the shore, and their vast weight, they make a deep impression, as if a heavy beam had been drawn along the sands.

Those whose employment it is to hunt them observe the track by which they are most frequently accustomed to go, and fix into the ground several pieces of wood, armed with sharp iron spikes, which they cover with the sand in such a manner as not to be perceptible. When therefore the animals make their way towards the places they usually haunt, they are wounded by these instruments, and speedily killed.

...The flesh also of the animal is sold at a dear rate, being thought to have a higher flavour than other kinds of meat, and by all persons it is esteemed a delicacy."-- Travels of Marco Polo[30]

This seems like a description of what we now call a dinosaur. And the answer to our question is, it appears that dinosaur meat was not only good to eat, it was an expensive delicacy. This also indicates you may not need to go very far back in time to find a dinosaur, or find a time when the unique conditions needed to preserve dinosaur tracks existed. We may be talking thousands of years instead of millions of years.

More Facts from China

When looking at the past we tend to be very Eurocentric. However, if a catastrophic event such as a global flood actually happened, you would expect there to be evidence around the world, including cultural evidence. It turns out there is. Nearly every culture has a flood story:

Inca in Peru: "They said that the water rose above the highest mountains in the world, so that all people and all created things

---

[30] https://tinyurl.com/y3a3atc5

Beginner's Guide To Tracking Dinosaurs

perished. No living thing escaped except a man and a woman, who floated in a box on the face of the waters and so were saved."

Bahnar - Cochin, China: the rivers swelled "till the waters reached the sky, and all living beings perished except two, a brother and a sister, who were saved in a huge chest. They took with them into the chest a pair of every sort of animal..."

Aztecs: "When mankind were overwhelmed with the deluge, none were preserved but a man named Coxcox ... and a woman called Xochiquetzal, who saved themselves in a little bark, and having afterwards got to land upon a mountain called by them Colhuacan, had there a great many children; ... these children were all born dumb, until a dove from a lofty tree imparted to them languages, but differing so much that they could not understand one another."

The Bible: "Now Noah was six hundred years old when the flood of water came upon the earth. Then Noah and his sons and his wife and his sons' wives with him entered the ark because of the water of the flood. Of clean animals and animals that are not clean and birds and everything that creeps on the ground, there went into the ark to Noah by twos, male and female, as God had commanded Noah. It came about after the seven days, that the water of the flood came upon the earth. In the six hundredth year of Noah's life, in the second month, on the seventeenth day of the month, on the same day all the fountains of the great deep burst open, and the floodgates of the sky were opened. The rain fell upon the earth for forty days and forty nights." – Genesis 7:6-12

Over time, oral histories tend to become garbled and embellished. So how do we know the written Biblical account is correct, and the oral Aztec version (and all other versions) is a garbled version of the Biblical account?

The Mesopotamian Gilgamesh Epic

It is often claimed the Bible copied its flood account from the Gilgamesh flood story. However, we know that cannot be true. Of all the flood stories, the Biblical account is the only one that is realistic and coherent. For example, the boat used in the Gilgamesh story is a cube 20 cubits square. That is a highly unstable shape that would tumble about in the water. No one inside such a "boat" would survive. Noah's Ark, on the other hand, had a dimensional

Are Dinosaurs Good To Eat?

ratio that is now known to be the best design for stability, and is the ratio we now use for all large ships. In a study done in the 1990's, and published in 1994,[31] the safety of the Ark was investigated and rated as superior, in high winds and waves, to all other hull shapes studied. Of all the flood stories, the Biblical account is the only one that describes a vessel that could survive a global flood.

The Ancient Chinese Written Record

People orally passed on the story about the flood for generations. However, the Chinese, with their pictograph writing, did something unique. The creator God of the Bible, and the flood, were such a big part of the lives of the original Chinese people that they incorporated them into their written language.

Figure 29 – The ancient Chinese character for large boat

Pictures are used for written Chinese. However, that does not mean each "word" is a unique character. Many of the characters are composed of other, smaller characters. The above is the ancient Chinese pictograph for a large boat (or ship). It is composed of three characters: the characters for boat, the character for number eight, and the character for mouth, representing living, breathing people. That's Noah's ark! Noah's ark was a large boat with eight people on board. We see the global flood and Noah's ark captured in ancient Chinese characters, providing cultural proof the flood was real.

---

[31] https://tinyurl.com/y47lxtbx

Beginner's Guide To Tracking Dinosaurs

There are many examples of Biblical truth recorded in the design of ancient Chinese characters. Here is another one:

Figure 30 – The ancient Chinese character for the word "garden" depicts the Garden of Eden.

The Word for Garden (or park).

In figure 30 we see that the ancient Chinese character for "garden" gives us a picture of the Garden of Eden. It includes an enclosure, and inside that enclosure is dust, breath (life), and two people. What we are seeing in this character is the creation of humanity out of dust in the Garden of Eden.

The character for "mouth" has several shades of meaning. Here it refers to breath... God took dust (Genesis 2:7) and breathed life into it. This character can also represent a living person, as it does with the character for a ship. One mouth (breathing) means one living person. However, there is another symbol for a person, and that symbol appears twice as a part of the symbol for garden, indicating two people... and one person is coming out of the side of the other. You can see this better in the contemporary character (on the right in figure 30) that has the same meaning. Draw a vertical line down the middle of this character and you can see there is the same character back-to-back. The complete story told here is; in an enclosed area (the garden of Eden) dust and breath (God breathed life into dust to give life to Adam), resulted in two people.

What Does This Have To Do With Tracking Dinosaurs?

If you plan to go back in time, track down a dinosaur, and photograph it (or eat it), you need to know how far back in time to go. If you go back too far, let's say so far that you are going to a point in

Are Dinosaurs Good To Eat?

time when nothing existed. What would happen? You would pop into nothing where nothing exists. That cannot be good.

Knowing how and when dinosaur tracks were preserved will help us determine how far back in time you should go. And we are starting to see an answer. Noah's flood, about 4,500 years ago, is looking more and more like the event that preserved dinosaur tracks.

As you saw in the previous chapter, there are many other unanswered questions about dinosaur tracks. As we put the pieces of this puzzle together, it is looking like Noah's flood is the answer. It is the explanation that solves all of the mysteries in a way that is both Biblically and scientifically sound. However, we need to understand what the conditions during Noah's flood were actually like. Let's look into that in the next chapter.

CHAPTER 11
PRESERVATION OF DINOSAUR TRACKS

The basic question that must be answered is: Why were billions of dinosaur tracks preserved as fossils, yet today we do not see any process that could result in the preservation of even a few footprints (or raindrops)? The present is obviously not the key to the past. Something big happened that we do not see happening today, and it resulted in billions of dinosaur footprints around the world preserved as fossils.

The most popular theory is that dinosaurs walked on a lakeshore where an annual flood buried and preserved their footprints. Do we see that happening anywhere today? No.

The Nile Delta region (Egypt) is an area famous for flooding annually, bringing new soil and resulting in conditions that are some of the best in the world for farming. This has been going on for thousands of years. Yet no footprints were preserved in these annual floods.

Evolution-based thinking theorizes that the location where our dinosaur tracks came from (the Connecticut River Valley) had an arid climate with an annual monsoon season that produced temporary lakes. Dinosaurs left footprints on the shores of the lakes and they fossilized. There are numerous Asian countries that have a monsoon season and a dry season… but no fossils are formed.

Preservation of Dinosaur Tracks

In the American west it is theorized that dinosaurs were walking on the western shore of an inland sea, leaving footprints that fossilized. Hudson's Bay and the Baltic Sea are inland seas. However, no fossils are produced on the shores of either of these. HOWEVER, some say the right type of inland seas only form during periods of high sea levels that have only existed in the past. That does not help. The thinking on sea levels is that sea levels were low during the early Jurassic when many hundreds of millions of dinosaur tracks where made. That is not the answer. Something very different was happening. In addition, it was big, it was worldwide. Something the world had never experienced before nor after.

Briefly Exposed Diluvial Sediments (BEDS)

All of the suggestions for what might have happened ignore the only written record we have of that time period. The Bible. In Genesis chapter seven the Bible records a world-wide, year-long flood as a historical event. Would such a global flood result in the conditions needed to produce fossil dinosaur footprints? Let's find out.

Some people think of Noah's Flood as being similar to filling a bathtub with water. A slow and steady rising water level. However, that is not realistic.

Michael Oard has developed a theory that seems realistic. It is called Briefly Exposed Deluvial Sediments, or simply BEDS. It describes a catastrophic event, driven by the fountains of the deep opening, volcanoes, runaway tectonic plate subduction, and massive earthquakes. BEDS postulates that, because of variations in the earth's surface and the varying geological energy released in different locations, there were local areas that were submerged, covered by sediment, and then they re-emerged for a short time. He writes,

> "All the dinosaur data can be explained by their final hours or days being spent on the freshly laid-and-then-exposed flat Flood sediments. Horizontal beds of wet, unlithified [still soft] sediment would have been ideal for the preservation of tracks, as they were uncovered by a local, temporary drop in relative sea level.
>
> Sea level would be oscillating considerably during the flood... There are at least five mechanisms that would have caused a brief and local fall in sea level. These include:

1. Tectonic uplifts or subsidence of the BEDS area;
2. Tsunamis;
3. Lunar tides;
4. Slow uplift or sinking of the crust in areas far from BEDS; and
5. The dynamics of Flood currents on shallow, large areas.[32]"

Solid Ground to Stand On

Imagine a global flood. The water is filled with sediment, more like a thick slurry than water. Locally the water levels are going up and down with the tides, storm waves, the movement of the earth's crust, and tsunamis. You are a dinosaur treading water. The water level is dropping, and your feet touch bottom. The water goes down further and you are standing on a fresh layer of sediment! Ahhh, you can rest. Walk around. This even provides an opportunity to quickly lay your eggs.

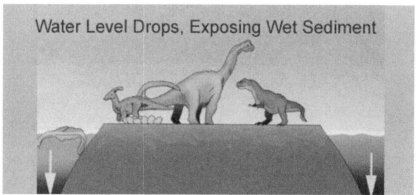

Figure 31 – A locally dropping water level exposes solid ground.

Maybe in a few hours, possibly in a day or so, the water rises again and more sediment is deposited (figure 32). You are able to keep your head above water, but some of the smaller dinosaurs are too small. They float for a while, but cannot stay afloat long enough. They drown. Your footprints and recently laid eggs are buried as more sediment accumulates.

---

[32] Michael J. Oard, "Dinosaur Challenges and Mysteries," Creation Book Publishers, (2011) page 115-116

Preservation of Dinosaur Tracks

The Water Level Drops Again

Once again the water level decreases (figure 33). It does not go down as far it was before, but there is a new layer of sediment and in a short time your feet are on solid ground. You are standing on a widespread, flat plain of dense mud that goes as far as the eye can see. This is fresh sediment, there is no vegetation. Just mud that goes on and on.

Figure 32 – The water rises again, drowning some dinosaurs and burying tracks and eggs in a fresh layer of sediment.

Figure 33 – The water level decreases once again, exposing the fresh layer of sediment on which the dinosaurs make more tracks and, in some locations, lay more eggs.[33]

---

[33] Figures 31-33 are from Michael Oard's book "Dinosaur Challenges and Mysteries." (Used with permission). I highly recommend this book. It shows that the global flood makes sense in light of the track, nest, egg and scavenged bones evidence.

Beginner's Guide To Tracking Dinosaurs

Or maybe the water level does not go down all the way, but your feet are touching the ground. You are standing in a couple of inches of water. The wind blown water is moving, creating ripples in the sediment.[34] Both your footsteps and the ripples are quickly buried as sediment carried by the shallow water settles out. Over a few hours, or maybe a day or so, the water rises and falls by several feet, continually depositing sediment. A few times the water level even drops far enough so that land appears, but soon water rolls across the surface once again, bringing more sediment.

This scenario not only produces the conditions that would result in the preservation and fossilization of dinosaur footprints, it describes the footprint patterns we see. Dinosaur footprints show they were walking, not running. In most locations the dinosaurs were not going in any specific direction. They appear to be moving slowly in random directions. Exactly what you would expect to see with dinosaurs on a flat mud plain with no food, and no reason to go in any particular direction.[35]

BEDS Answers All the Questions

A global flood and the BEDS theory answers all of our questions:

Why are billions of dinosaur tracks found on flat bedding planes, some of which extend over very large regions?[36] This is exactly what we would expect from a global flood. On a world-wide scale geology has shown us there are vast continent size layers of sediment.

Locally, where dinosaurs were gathered, a global flood would produce layer after layer of flat wet sediment. Those dinosaurs that could float, or were big enough to keep their heads above water, would walk in the mud, leaving their tracks to be quickly buried as the water rose again.

Why is there little or no evidence of vegetation, or food sources, where dinosaur tracks are found? The plants would have either been

---

[34] Dinosaur tracks are found in water rippled sediment.

[35] At some locations there appear to be dinosaur "trails" with most dinosaurs heading in one direction. This is what would be expected outside of a rift valley environment such as existed in the Connecticut River Valley, with the dinosaurs having the ability to move away from the rising water.

[36] Martin Lockley, "Tracking Dinosaurs," Cambridge University Press, (1991) page 7

Preservation of Dinosaur Tracks

buried or stripped off the land early in the flood. The tracks dinosaur left were made in fresh sedimentary mud flats, which were quickly buried in new sediment, with no time for vegetation to sprout in the fresh mud.

The Nash Dinosaur Track Quarry, where the tracks we are studying come from, is in a rift valley that is crossed by a range of east-west mountains called the Mt. Holyoke Range. The quarry is located on the south edge of this range. The mountains would have slowed, or at times blocked the flow of flood water, resulting in the quarry being in a backwater. Flood waters would have carried organic debris, such as small tree branches, into this area where they would settle into the accumulating sediment. That is why the quarry has unusually high levels of fossilized and coalified wood, but organic material such as this is rare at other dinosaur track locations.

Why are many tracksites dominated by carnivorous theropod dinosaurs? What were they eating? In a global flood situation, groups of animals would become isolated by the rising waters. In some cases they might be all herbivores, with no carnivores. In other cases there would be a mix of carnivores and herbivores. The hungry carnivores, in many cases, would eat almost all of the available herbivores, leaving just carnivores. As a result, overall we would expect to see, in some locations, track evidence of many carnivores and few herbivores.

Dinosaur tracks are found in marine environments, something the experts say is impossible.[37] For example, dinosaur footprints are found in sediment that also includes marine fossils. They are also found in dolomite, a type of limestone that only forms under special conditions under water. While dinosaurs did not walk on the ocean bottom, the ocean bottom, including marine life that later become fossilized, was taken up and carried as sediment onto the land as the flood waters rose and fell in places where dinosaurs did walk. In addition, dolomite layers, which form underwater by calcium carbonate replacement, may have been briefly exposed (BEDS) allowing dinosaurs to leave footprints in the dolomite (see footnote 33).

It is beginning to look like a global flood, just as described in the Bible, is the only option that provides a realistic explanation for all the evidence we see.

---

[37] https://answersingenesis.org/dinosaurs/footprints/fossilized-footprints-a-dinosaur-dilemma/

CHAPTER 12
THE TRACK EVIDENCE

Now let us examine the track evidence, all of the evidence, without assuming a conclusion. When we do that we will find that the only conditions that could result in the fossilization of dinosaur footprints were those of a global flood as described in the Bible.

Your Feet Do Not Make Fossil Footprints

Try the simple experiment I mentioned earlier. Go for a walk on the beach or through a mud puddle. You will leave footprints. Come back a few days or a week later. What will you find? Nothing. Your tracks will be gone. The most common claim about dinosaur tracks is that dinosaurs came to a lakeshore to drink, or maybe hunt herbivores. They left tracks. Those tracks hardened in the sun and were buried in the next annual flood. How often is that observed happening today? Zero. Nadda. It does not happen. No fossilized tracks.

Yet there are over a billion fossilized dinosaur tracks all over the world (except Antarctica)!

Making Fossilized Dinosaur Footprints – A Summary

For dinosaur footprints to be preserved, the following is required:

The Track Evidence

(1) The dinosaur needs to step in mud, or wet sand, such that its foot leaves an impression.

(2) The footprints must be buried gently, so they are not eroded by the flow the sediment laden water. For example, rapidly flowing water, or wave action, will wipe away the footprints. They must also be buried quickly and deeply to protect them from being destroyed by rain, weather, trampling by other animals, drying and crumbling, or other environmental conditions.

(3) The sediment must lithify, meaning to turn to stone. while retaining the footprint impression.

The Track Evidence - Connecticut River Valley

Let's look at real world evidence, dinosaur tracks from the Nash Quarry in the Connecticut River Valley. This is where our tracks came from (see Appendix B).

(a) As is true of other tracksites, the tracks are found on flat bedding planes with no signs of vegetation growing. That is not only unusual, it is weird. Flat mud plains, with no vegetation, for miles. For example, in the region where the dinosaur tracks we have come from, interstate highway construction and even home building routinely turns up dinosaur tracks. They are found along the Connecticut River for about 80 miles, and for more than 2-3/4 miles east of the river. All on what was flat, muddy ground with no signs of vegetation growing. Nothing like this is seen today.

(b) The fossilized vegetation at the Nash Quarry is unusual. It is mainly small branches and stems, and small roots. No leaves. No grasses. Moreover, it is broken into small pieces. It appears to be wood fragments that were carried in from somewhere else. As is typical of other track sites, there are no signs of vegetation growing.

The color of the shale indicates, in part, the amount of vegetation originally in the sediment.[38] Over time, the vegetation decomposes, leaving carbon. The darker the shale the higher the carbon

---

[38] This would be finely pulverized vegetation mixed in as a part of the sediment.

Beginner's Guide To Tracking Dinosaurs

content. Rocks from the Nash Quarry vary in color. A few layers are light brown sandstone, with little vegetation. Most of the layers are various shades of grey, with many of them being a dark gray shale, indicating a significant amount of pulverized vegetation was originally mixed into the sediment. This would not be locally growing vegetation. It was plant material carried in by the sediment laden flood waters.

(c) Dinosaur tracks are found in rippled sediment, indicating the dinosaur was walking in shallow moving water that created ripples. Tracks made by swimming dinosaurs, whose feet were just barely touching the bottom, are seen at Dinosaur State Park in Connecticut (about 50 miles south of the Nash Quarry).

(d) The tracks do not reveal hunting behavior, and for all practical purposes, there are no herbivore tracks. All carnivores. What did they eat? There usually needs to be a ratio of at least 10 to 15 herbivores for every carnivore. We do not see that. No one has actually counted, but the ratio is probably in the range of one herbivore track for every 100 to 150 carnivore tracks (per a conversation with Kornell Nash). It is claimed they ate fish and each other.

> "The apparent striking numerical dominance of carnivores that seems to be a violation of the basic trophic or Eltonian ecological pyramid may be real. The base of the food chain may have been largely aquatic as we will discuss at Stop 3 and 4, and the carnivorous dinosaurs may have primarily subsisted on fish and other carnivores that ate fish."[39] – Paul Olsen

However, in 80 years of digging fossils at the Nash Quarry, only a few very small fish fossils have been found in the deeper layers.

(e) At Nash's Quarry they have dug up tracks from about six vertical feet and thousands of fine, thin layers of sediment. Throughout all of the multiple layers of sediment the same type of tracks are found, layer after layer after layer. The quality varies as the quality of the sediment varies, but, as Kornell Nash answered when I asked him about where to look for tracks, *"It doesn't matter where I dig, there will be*

---

[39] Paul Olsen, "Dinosaur Dominance." Keck Geology Consortium 2017 Annual Meeting Wesleyan University

The Track Evidence

tracks." The same type of dinosaur was walking here while at least six feet of sediment built up.[40] Does that sound like a lake shore? That would be a very unusual lake.

(f) At Nash's mostly individual tracks are found. (This may have been the result of the quarrying method they used.) In general, tracks do not show a preferential direction. When trackways are found, they are straight, and there may have been a slight preference for a northwest direction[41].

None of this is normal. None of this is what we see happening today.

Evidence From Around the World

What do we notice about tracks around the world?

(a) Tracks are found on flat bedding plains with no vegetation.

(b) Trackways typically go in straight lines, and in most cases they do not have a preferred direction.

(c) Many track sites are dominated by carnivores, with few tracks made by herbivores.

(d) Some dinosaur tracks are found in sediment containing marine fossils and in sediments that only form underwater.

(e) Some dinosaur tracks are found in coal, which supposedly forms at the bottoms of swamps. Not a place a dinosaur could walk and leave footprints.

(f) Very few fossil tracks worldwide were made by dinosaurs with a body plan indicating they were poor swimmers. Fossilized tracks are made by dinosaurs that have a body plan indicating they had some ability to swim.

---

[40] Kornel Nash was just starting to dig into deeper layers when he passed away in 2019.
[41] From a personal conversation with Kornel Nash. I documented two trackways at the quarry. One went in a roughly NW direction. The other in a North Easterly direction.

Beginner's Guide To Tracking Dinosaurs

The Evidence Points to a Global Flood

The evidence points to a global flood that quickly deposited massive amounts of sediment. That would explain, for example, the flat bedding plains that go on for miles with no vegetation.

Looking at the evidence at Nash's Quarry, where we see six vertical feet of sediment all with the same dinosaur footprints. Is it normal for six feet of sediment to build up on a lake shore? No. What is observed is that as sediment is added to the shoreline, the lake becomes smaller. The dry land advances and the shoreline retreats toward the center of the lake. In addition, the conditions in which footprints can be made in mud only exist in a narrow strip along the shore. Too far away from the lake and the dirt is not wet enough. Too close and the mud is too soft. So as the sediment builds up year after year, what should be observed is a diagonal pattern of footprints through the vertical distance in the sediment, as the shoreline moved further into the lake. Instead what is seen is a water level that is moving straight upward in elevation as massive amounts of sediment were deposited simultaneously throughout the area. That could only happen as a result of a flood on the scale of the flood described in the Bible.

In addition, the fossil tracks are in nearly every layer, frequently overlapping the tracks above and below. If tracks were buried by annual floods, what would be observed would be a layer of tracks, then layers with no tracks (the sediment from the annual flood), then another layer of tracks resulting from dinosaurs walking around on the top of the new layers of sediment. Then the pattern would repeat. But, that is not what is observed.

Another question comes to mind. How long does it take to deposit six feet of thin layered sediment? Kornell Nash stated that the estimate was 20,000 to 25,000 years. Does a lakeshore remain stable, in the same location, with no vegetation, and with the same type of animal, and only that type of animal, continually walking on it, leaving footprints in every layer, for 20,000 years? Not likely. What matches the observed evidence is the sediment being deposited quickly, over a short time period, in a continuous process.

A global flood also explains why there is no vegetation. If dinosaur tracks were preserved by annual local floods, there should be some evidence of vegetation growing. Plants take root quickly. Even

The Track Evidence

concrete sidewalks require continual maintenance to keep the vegetation out. All it takes is a tiny crack and something sprouts. With a Biblical flood the sediment would be accumulating too quickly for vegetation to sprout.[42]

At Nash's, as well as many other tracksites, the dinosaurs are not heading in a specific direction. If they were coming to a lake to drink or fish, you would think the tracks would show them coming and going back and forth from the lake. Instead, the tracks indicate aimless wandering, as though there was no reason to go in any specific direction… such as when there is nothing but flat mud in every direction.

Why so many carnivores and few herbivores? In Biblical flood conditions the carnivores would eat all of the available herbivores. The rising waters would isolate groups of dinosaurs, some of which would have included carnivores. The result would be that all the locally available herbivores would be eaten, leaving only carnivores as we see in the footprint record.

The dinosaur track evidence points toward a global flood, as described in the Bible. However, before we jump to a conclusion, let's examine other types of evidence.

---

[42] Mount St. Helens showed the "life began to appear on the landscape almost immediately after the eruption." https://tinyurl.com/yy5l8d7y

CHAPTER 13
FOSSIL DINOSAUR EGGS

Like dinosaur tracks, dinosaur eggs provide powerful evidence that a Biblical global flood is real and actually happened. Let's start with an important question few people ask:

Were Fossil Dinosaur Eggs Laid Normally?

"Eggs were everywhere. As we strode across the mud-cracked flats exposed beneath the banded ridges of crimson rock that radiated under the searing Patagonian sun, crew members began kneeling down to examine small, dark gray fragments of rounded rock with a curious texture. We knew immediately from the distinctive texture that we had found something startling--dinosaur eggs.[43]"

"Dinosaur eggshells, whole eggs, clutches of eggs, and even baby dinosaur bones have proven to be more common than was previously realized... It is clear that dinosaur eggs and baby bones have been found on almost every continent except Antarctica. I suspect that they will eventually be found there as well.[44]"

Notice one word that is not used... "nests." The word "clutch" simply refers to a group of eggs, not a nest.

---

[43] Luis Chiappe and Lowell Dingus, "Walking On Eggs," Scribner (2001), page 23

[44] Kenneth Carpenter, "Eggs, Nests, and Baby Dinosaurs," Indiana University Press, (1999) page 8

Fossil Dinosaur Eggs

Millions of dinosaur eggs have been found, along with huge amounts of broken eggs and eggshell. In one area in Spain, for example, it is estimated there are 300,000 eggs. This abundance of dinosaur eggs, all laid out in the open, should have resulted in a question: Were dinosaur eggs laid normally? The evolutionary assumption is yes. This assumption is accepted as true, so the question is never asked. However, a review of the evidence makes it clear it is a question that needs to be answered.

Basics about Dinosaur Eggs

Let's say you wanted to own a dinosaur egg. You go to EBay and notice there are several for sale. You pick what looks like a good one, and a few days later you have a dinosaur egg... that is most likely a fake from China. It happens all the time. What do you need to know about real dinosaur eggs?

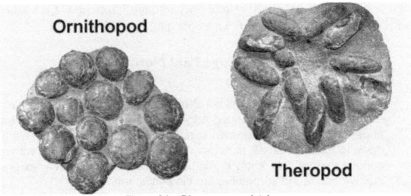
Figure 34 – Dinosaur egg clutches.

Dinosaur eggs have two basic shapes. There are the round ones that were laid by sauropods and ornithopods, and there are elongated eggs laid by dinosaurs such as theropods.

As mentioned in the quote on the previous page, dinosaur eggs have a texture. They are not smooth like chicken eggs. Figure 35 shows a replica theropod egg we have in our museum. You can clearly see the texture.

The specific type of dinosaur that laid the egg cannot be identified, because it is rare to find dinosaur eggs with embryos inside. It is also extremely rare to find fossil bones near dinosaur eggs. Eggs

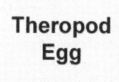

Figure 35 – Notice the surface texture of a theropod egg.

are found out in the open, on flat sediment surfaces, with little or no evidence of vegetation. And there is little fossil evidence (make that essentially none) that the dinosaur that laid the eggs stayed with their eggs.

In addition, not all eggs are in clutches. Individual eggs are found scattered around between clutches. Chiappe and Dingus write about the eggs they found in Patagonia:

> "Other dinosaurs laid their eggs in a spiral pattern within a nest. Still others laid their eggs in rather poorly defined patterns within a nest, and some laid them randomly across an area without a nest.[45]"

In this instance, the term "nest" is used. That does not mean there actually was a nest. Some paleontologists assume that clutches of eggs, with no nest structure, must be the normal way dinosaur laid eggs. So they refer to them as a "nest" even though there is no evidence of an actual nest. They are assuming there must be a nest. However, that is not what is observed.

Dinosaur eggs are often found in localized areas in which clutches are close together, often in multiple sediment layers, with individual eggs scattered about. In only a couple of instances have there been reports in which evidence, usually a change in the color of the sediment, for a nest structure has been inferred. Not observed, but inferred.

---

[45] Luis Chiappe and Lowell Dingus, "Walking On Eggs," Scribner (2001), page 87

Fossil Dinosaur Eggs

How Were Dinosaur Eggs Preserved and Fossilized?

The question of dinosaur egg preservation and fossilization is similar to that for dinosaur footprints. Eggs must be quickly and deeply buried, in this case to protect them from predators. However, the flow of water carrying the sediment must be gentle so as not to break or move the eggs. Let's think about this. To get enough sediment to quickly and deeply bury eggs (two or three feet of sediment is required for this) requires an energetic water flow that can even erode rock quickly. Based on the present being the key to the past, that means a flash flood type of flow. That is what it takes today to produce a lot of sediment. However, an energetic flash flood will move and break the eggs. Therefore, it is not an option. We do not see any mechanism operating today that could bury, preserve, and fossilize eggs.

Here is another interesting piece of evidence: Some dinosaur eggs have been found in marine strata. Carpenter writes,

> "One of the oddest occurrences of an egg is from the Mooreville Chalk of Alabama. This chalk was deposited in the northern end of the proto-Gulf of Mexico. How this egg came to rest on the bottom of the sea is unknown.[46]"

Other eggs have been found in sediment containing marine fossils, but chalk forms underwater. Dinosaurs do not lay eggs underwater, and eggs are too fragile to have been carried there by a flood. Maybe they were carried in floating vegetation? Seems far-fetched.

Don't Stop Until You Have the Complete Story

Pathological Eggs: The formation of an egg is a complicated process that takes place within the dinosaur. The last step is putting the hard shell on the egg. Then it is stored in the mother's body until all of the eggs can be laid. If the mother is under stress and is prevented from laying the eggs, some of the eggs may have pathologies, meaning they are not normal. A common pathology is multiple shells. If the egg is unable to be moved into the storage area in the lower uterus, and it stays in the shell making area of the uterus, a second

---

[46] Kenneth Carpenter, "Eggs, Nests, and Baby Dinosaurs," Indiana University Press, (1999) page 19

shell will form. Only the most recent eggs to form within the mother would have this pathology. When dinosaur eggs are examined using an electron microscope these multiple shells can sometimes be detected. In one example 10% of fossil dinosaur eggs were found to have multiple shells. That is far in excess of what is common under normal conditions.

> "Abnormal, multilayered eggshells are frequently reported in fossil specimens. Excavation of one clutch exposed 30 eggs, distributed in three levels, including 27 normal eggs and 3 multilayered eggs. The three abnormal eggs occupied the highest level within the clutch and represent the last eggs laid by the female sauropod.[47]"

> "This abnormal condition often results from physiologic or environmental "stress" and prolonged egg retention by the female. A similar condition found in fossil dinosaur eggshell from France was purported to result from environmental stress associated with the Cretaceous extinction event.[48]"

Many Eggs Have Not Hatched:

We cannot help notice that the dinosaur clutch replicas in our museum, as well as the clutches we have seen in other museums, have mostly unhatched, unbroken eggs. Kenneth Carpenter writes,

> "A surprising number of whole dinosaur eggs are known, especially the big, spherical Megaloolithus eggs from France, India and Argentina. Why these eggs failed to hatch is a subject of much speculation.[49]"

The conclusion that makes sense is that they were buried before they could hatch.

There is possible evidence for a few hatched eggs in that some fossil dinosaur eggs are broken on top, with no egg shell fragments found inside. It is assumed this indicates the shell was broken from

---

[47] Jackson, Garrido, Schmitt, Chiappe, Dingus, and Loope, "Abnormal, Multilayered Titanosaur Eggs from in situ Clutches at the Auca Mahuevo locality, Neuquén Province, Argentina," Journal of Vertebrate Paleontology v24, 10/12/2004

[48] .Jackson, Schweitzer and Schmitt, "Dinosaur Eggshell Study Using Scanning Electron Microscopy" Scanning, 01/09/2006

[49] Kenneth Carpenter, "Eggs, Nests, and Baby Dinosaurs," Indiana University Press, (1999) page 119

Fossil Dinosaur Eggs

the inside. Is this a valid assumption? I just ran a simple experiment. I cracked open the top of a chicken egg and sucked out the contents. No shell fragments were left inside. So broken tops could be a sign of predators. Also, Michael Oard reports that, *"Many of the broken top eggs have shells within the egg.[50]"* This would indicate the tops of the eggs were broken by something other than hatching, such as sediment compaction or a predator.

Traces of Protein Found In Dinosaur Eggs

Schweitzer, et.al in a paper titled "Molecular Preservation in Late Cretaceous Sauropod Dinosaur Eggshells" reported detecting protein in fossil dinosaur egg shells. This is very interesting because proteins degrade rapidly and certainly do not last millions of years. It is an indication fossil dinosaur eggs are not all that old.

Like dinosaur footprints, what we see in dinosaur eggs are numerous mysteries. There are many aspects of fossil dinosaur eggs that do not make sense; no nest structures; eggs scattered about; no sign of dinosaurs staying with their eggs; many eggs have not hatched; numerous pathological eggs, eggs laid in flat bedding planes with no vegetation. We do not see conditions today, nor do we see anywhere outside of the Bible a record of conditions in the past that could fossilize dinosaur eggs… especially in the huge numbers we find.

---

[50] Dinosaur Challenges and Mysteries, page 105.

CHAPTER 14
DINOSAUR EGG EVIDENCE

Fossilization: Millions of Years?

No eggs are being fossilized today. Not reptile eggs. Nor crocodile eggs. Nor any type of egg, even when buried in mud or vegetation. No remains of eggs, such as broken egg shell or hatched eggs, are being fossilized today.

We should take a break here to mention that fossilization does not take millions of years. The process of fossilization is happening today. What we do not see are animal tracks being fossilized. Nor are eggs or egg shell being fossilized.

> "Exceptionally preserved sauropod eggshells discovered in Upper Cretaceous (Campanian) deposits in Patagonia, Argentina, contain skeletal remains and soft tissues of embryonic Titanosaurid dinosaurs. To preserve these labile embryonic remains, the rate of mineral precipitation must have superseded post-mortem degradative processes, resulting in virtually instantaneous mineralization of soft tissues.[51]"

[Note: Embryos have few hard parts. They decay away to nothing very quickly. That means they must fossilize very quickly.]

---

[51] Schweitzer, Chiappe, Garrido, Lowenstein, and Pincus, "Molecular Preservation in Late Cretaceous Sauropod Dinosaur Eggshells," Proceedings Biological Sciences, April 22, 2005

Dinosaur Egg Evidence

In other words, mineralization (the creation of a fossil) happened virtually instantaneously, meaning in days or weeks, not millions of years.

In his 1989 article published in the journal Geology Today, David Martill describes how, under the right conditions, egg

> "...lithification was instantaneous and fossilization may have even been the cause of death.[52]"

It does not take millions of years, or even thousands of years, for fossils to form. What is needed that is not happening today? The answer: rapid burial deeply in sediment with the necessary chemical properties. Rapid and deep, yet gentle burial is required to preserve an egg from scavengers, weathering, and other forces that might damage it. That is not happening today. It has not happened throughout history, except during the global flood described in Genesis in the Bible.

The answer to the question on the previous page, "Were fossil dinosaur eggs laid normally?" is, no. The evidence points to the existence of very unusual conditions.

Let's Summarize the Evidence

(1) Many fossil dinosaur eggs were laid in clutches, but not nests. Some were laid as individual eggs, scattered about. There is no strong evidence that fossil eggs were laid in nests. It looks like the dinosaurs were under stress, they had to lay their eggs to get rid of them, and move on.

(2) Fossil dinosaur eggs were laid on extensive flat bedding plains -- flat expanses of mud or wet sand -- with no vegetation.

(3) Clutches, with associated individual eggs scattered about, are close together, and have been found in multiple sediment levels in the same location.

(4) There is no strong evidence that dinosaurs remained with their eggs. They laid the eggs and moved on (or floated away).

---

[52] D.M. Martill, "The Medusa Effect: Instantaneous Fossilization," Geology Today 5, 1989

Beginner's Guide To Tracking Dinosaurs

(5) Pathological eggs with multiple shells are much more common than they should be, indicating the dinosaurs were under stress.

(6) Eggs have been found in marine deposits, with some eggs found in deposits that could only form underwater.

(7) Eggs are subject to predators, and had to have been buried deeply and quickly in order to protect them.

(8) Eggs are fragile and needed to be buried gently, otherwise they will be broken or washed away.

(9) Many of the eggs had not hatched, indicating they were buried, and in some cases almost instantly fossilized, before they could hatch.

(10) In some cases huge numbers of eggs are found in one location, such as an estimated 300,000 at a location in France.

(11) For fossilization to occur there had to be water carrying a heavy load of sediment, of the correct chemical composition, that could accomplish fast, deep, yet gentle burial over a wide area.

It is obvious that this is not painting a picture of conditions that exist today. What past events could provide the conditions that meet all of these criteria?

The Answer: Briefly Exposed Diluvial Sediments (BEDS)

BEDS provides a reasonable description of what may have happened during the Biblical global flood. Please note that, although the illustration (figure 36) shows a tiny island, it is just an illustration. Areas of hundreds of square miles were probably exposed in some cases

Dinosaur Egg Evidence

Figure 36 – Briefly Exposed Diluvial Sediments

A global flood, as described in the Bible, would result in all of the above. As water washed over the land inundating and then retreating from the land, as the result of tides, weather, uplifts, earthquakes, and geological events, all the while continually rising higher, vast flat areas would be covered with sediment with no vegetation. Exactly what we see in the rock record.

With the water rising, the earth shaking, and dry land disappearing, dinosaurs would be stressed to the max. They would be holding in their eggs, waiting for normal conditions... until they could wait no longer. There was nothing to use to build a nest, and the eggs had to come out. Some dinosaurs laid their eggs in the mud in their normal pattern. Others laid eggs as they walked along. A few tried to build a somewhat normal nest by mounding up mud. However, in the end, the eggs were laid. The last couple of eggs laid with multiple shells. And the dinosaurs moved on, seeking food or avoiding the rising waters. The eggs were quickly buried as the next surge of water brought more sediment. However, not necessarily all eggs.

A few dinosaurs probably laid their eggs in a location where they had time to hatch before the next wave of sediment laden water came in. As a result of stress they had held the eggs in much longer than normal, and the embryos were already well developed before the egg was laid. As a result the incubation time was short and they hatched quickly... or in some cases the eggs with well developed embryos were buried by a new layer of sediment and fossilized.

The present is not the key to the past. The physical evidence shows the past was very different and that is why we have things such as fossil footprints and fossilized eggs that we do not see happening today. The key to understanding the past is the eyewitness record of the Bible.

Objection to Gentle, Rapid Burial

How could a catastrophic global flood, with earthquakes, volcanoes, and massive earth movements gently bury dinosaur footprints and eggs?

Just as the picture of water slowly rising in a bathtub is not a correct overall view of the flood, so also violent tsunamis crashing into the land is not an accurate portrayal of the flood in every location. Yes, there were massive tsunamis that pulverized rock into fine sediment. However, there were also locations that, for a time, would have experienced much gentler conditions. Imagine mud flats that go on for miles in every direction. A tsunami crashes into the shore far away. However, as the water rolls over maybe hundreds of miles of mud flats, it loses energy becoming a gentle, but still massive flow of water that slowly increases in depth and then subsides. In addition, for a time rift valleys, mountains, and geological uplift would shield local areas from the direct impact of the crashing waters. Overall, there would be areas violently torn up, and other areas that, for a time, had gentler water level changes.

Tracks and Eggs: Powerful Evidence

The question is simple. What scenario best fits the dinosaur track and egg evidence we observe? Only a global flood as described in the Bible.

The geological, climate and other processes we see operating today, do not provide reasonable explanations for the fossilization of dinosaur tracks and eggs. The slow erosional processes we see today could never have produced sufficient sediment to bury and protect dinosaur tracks and eggs quickly and deeply and around the world. The ratio of carnivore tracks to herbivore tracks does not describe a long-term sustainable situation, but instead is a picture of extinction. Eggs laid out in the open, with no protection, is not survivable. Dinosaur tracks and eggs on flat bedding plains that go on for miles, with no vegetation, describe conditions that never existed... except during the global flood.

Dinosaur Egg Evidence

There is no other explanation. The Bible says there was a global flood. Such a flood was a huge physical event that would leave behind evidence. And it did. Evidence we see in dinosaur tracks and eggs. For additional evidences, I refer you to our Science Pastor web site where you will find short videos and web pages describing other physical evidence that a global flood really happened.

www.SciencePastor.com/flood

CHAPTER 15
FALSE PRESUPPOSITIONS

Figure 37 – How big was T-Rex? Is this a life-size T-Rex?

This A Life-Size T-Rex

The above is a picture of a life-size model of a T-Rex we have in our museum. It is about 20 inches tall at the hip. Am I telling a story, or is this truly a life-size T-Rex?

Life-Size T-Rex?

Yes, our T-Rex is life-size. This is a life-size reproduction of a juvenile T-Rex. We make assumptions based on past experience. Every time we read about T-Rex, or see a T-Rex in a movie, they are huge... and hungry. As a result, the picture we have in our minds is that of a huge and powerful two-legged dinosaur. However, like you,

False Presuppositions

a T-Rex started out as a baby. The largest dinosaur egg is about the size of a football. In fact, there is a bird egg that is larger than the biggest dinosaur egg (the Elephant Bird).

Wrong Presuppositions

Presuppositions are important. We would have a difficult time getting through the day without presuppositions. By presupposing that something is true or false, we can deal with it without thinking. For example, if someone takes a pot off a stove and pours you a cup of coffee, your presupposition will be that it is hot. You will start by sipping the coffee, not gulping. That coffee is hot is a presupposition that eliminates the need to evaluate whether or not each cup of coffee is hot. We use presuppositions all the time, and that is a good thing.

However, at times our presuppositions can be wrong. It may be because of what we were taught, or a presupposition can be based on a wrong assumption, such as every T-Rex in the movies is big, so all T-Rexes must be big. Wrong presuppositions can lead to a wrong understanding of the world we live in. That can cause serious problems.

An important presupposition is that the present is the key to the past. We assume that everything has always been as we see it now. That is a presupposition that leads to major errors in thinking. As we have already seen with dinosaur fossil footprints and eggs, the present is not the key to the past. Only when we realize that everything has not always been as we see it today, and there was a global flood as described in the Bible, do we get a picture that matches the fossil evidence we see today.

A presupposition can be difficult to change. In many instances, a presupposition supports other beliefs. Giving up the presupposition means giving up a long-held, cherished belief. We do not like that. However, no matter how much we wish it did, what we like or are comfortable with, does not define reality.

Here Comes Evolution

The presupposition that evolution is true distorts our thinking in many other areas, including our understanding of scripture. In the next chapters we will be looking at some of the icons of evolution.

Beginner's Guide To Tracking Dinosaurs

These are supposed examples of evolution that are firmly believed and held out as examples of evolution actually having happened. For example, in their book "Contested Bones" Christopher Rupe and Dr. John Sanford write about the problem of fossils that are physically dated to be older than what is compatible with a belief in evolution. The result is that the physical evidence is thrown out, and dates are changed to be compatible with evolutionary beliefs. In other words, ignore the evidence in order to sustain the belief. That is not science!

They note that in the end some fossils cannot be accepted for what they obviously are:

> "The reason has everything to do with scientific politics and deeply entrenched evolutionary presuppositions.[53]"

> "When it comes to the field of paleoanthropology, the fossil evidence has always been interpreted in light of the evolutionary view of human history. The ape-to-man story did not arise by scientific observations, it arose as a philosophically driven speculation, based on Darwin's writings… It is from within this ape-to-man framework that the paleo-community now admits they cannot make 'evolutionary sense' of the hominin fossils. We suggest that the reason they have this problem is because they are interpreting the fossils in light of a flawed ideological presupposition."[54]

We will talk about the fossils in the section on human evolution, but the point is that, strongly held presuppositions can overrule reality. If you are going to track and hunt dinosaurs, your life depends on accepting, and dealing with reality, not what some people wish was reality.

The question is; are you going to stick with presuppositions that have proven to be false, or are you willing to learn and follow the evidence wherever it leads? Evolution is one of, if not the most powerful presupposition that exists today. However, it is not supported by science, nor the evidence, nor the Bible.

---

[53] Christopher Rupe and Dr. John Sanford, "Contested Bones", FMS Publications, (2019) page 139
[54] Ibid page 340

False Presuppositions

CHAPTER 16
DINOSAURS BECAME BIRDS?
JUST WISHFUL THINKING!

When you are tracking a dinosaur, should you expect to come to the end of the trail and find a bird? No! The hypothesis that a dinosaur, commonly said to be a Troolodon dinosaur, gradually made millions of changes to its DNA, to became all birds is absurd.

Dinosaur to Bird?

What is the evidence that dinosaurs evolved to become birds?

#1 - Dinosaurs lay eggs, and birds lay eggs with some similar attributes. This means we have two types of animals, plus reptiles and the platypus, that lay eggs for reproduction.

#2 - Soft tissue and collagen[55] has been found in T-Rex dinosaur bones, proving that dinosaurs did not die out millions of years ago.

---

[55] Finding soft tissue (as well as red blood cells) should have ended the discussion. Even evolutionary scientists know that soft tissue cannot last millions of years. Yet they say they know dinosaur fossils are over 65 million years old. Even though it does not make sense, they "know" this soft tissue somehow lasted more than 65 million years. The conclusion is 100% based on assuming evolution is true. (continued)

When some of the component amino acids of that soft tissue (amino acids are used to make proteins), were compared with amino acids in the collagen in present-day animals,

Dinosaurs Became Birds? Just Wishful Thinking

Believers in bird evolution say that because the collagen proteins, when compared to other animals, matches that of birds better than any other animal, then birds must have evolved from dinosaurs. Of course, this is 100% based on the assumption evolution happened.

#3 - Birds have feathers and dinosaurs... well... they do not have feathers unless you have a good imagination. According to bird expert Larry Martin, what are interpreted as feather traces on dinosaurs are actually frayed collagen fibers. Feather expert Alan Brush (UCONN, Storrs, CT), states that they *"lack the organization found in modern feathers."*[56]

#4 - Some dinosaurs, such as velociraptors, had small bones that move the ribs and sternum to help breathing. These bones are similar to bones in diving birds, meaning the dinosaur was starting to evolve into a bird. On the other hand, the dinosaur may have been designed to do things that required a greater respiration ability, such as running fast.

#5 - Theropod dinosaurs are bipedal, they walk on two feet, and birds walk on two feet... and so do people.

This is not a very strong case for birds evolving from dinosaurs. These similarities might be because dinosaurs and birds had a common designer. In addition, concluding this is evidence for evolution does not take into account the many major differences between birds and dinosaurs, as well as the impossibility of such dramatic physiological (and genetic) changes. But, wait! There is more! There is a transitional fossil. Archaeopteryx!

Most experts now agree that archaeopteryx was a bird, or possibly a mosaic. It is no longer thought of as a transitional fossil. We should not even need to talk about it. However, icons of evolution die hard, and it may be decades before these facts are universally recognized. So, let us talk about archaeopteryx.

---

they saw some similarity and proclaimed this is proof of evolution. However, all life is carbon-based and uses many of the same proteins. It is reasonable to find two different animals having very similar collagen proteins.

[56] https://creation.com/dino-bird-evolution-falls-flat

Beginner's Guide To Tracking Dinosaurs

Archaeopteryx is a BIRD!

By the way, what is a mosaic?

A mosaic is an animal that combines the physical characteristics of several different animals. The best-known mosaic is the platypus. Its fur covered body looks like a mammal, but it also has characteristics of birds and reptiles. For example, it suckles its young, a mammal characteristic. It lays reptile-like eggs, and has webfeet and a bill like a duck. Let's not forget the claws, one of which is poisonous. The platypus must be a transition between reptiles and... well, something else. Nope. It is just a platypus and was never anything else.

There is nothing in the fossil record that indicates the platypus was anything other than a platypus. It is categorized as a monotreme, a mammal that lays reptile-like eggs and suckles their young. It is unique. The only animal in its category. The platypus is a mosaic, meaning it has a combination of characteristics found in other, unrelated animals.

Looking at birds, an interesting one is the South American bird called a Hoatzin. Their young have claws on their wings, they are expert underwater swimmers, and they eat and digest grass like a cow. That is an odd bird... but it is real. God, in designing His creation, is not limited by human created categories.

> **Key Point:**
>
> God is not restricted to creating within categories established by humans.

Dinosaurs Became Birds? Just Wishful Thinking

What Is Phylogeny?

Phylogeny is the study of the evolutionary history of a species or group of organisms, such as birds. It creates lines of descent showing the supposed evolutionary relationships of organisms based on common or similar characteristics. It is an attempt to trace the evolutionary history of all living organisms.

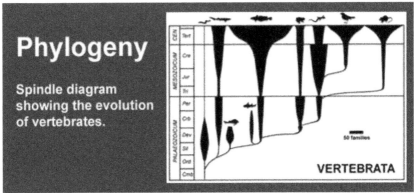

Figure 38 – Spindle diagram showing evolutionary "relationships"

Phylogenetic studies result in diagrams, called phylogenetic trees, showing the evolutionary relationships between organisms. The one shown above is one of the simpler diagrams called a spindle diagram. It is also known as a bubble diagram or a romerogram. Time is shown on the vertical axis. The width of each column indicates the diversity of individuals through time.

Another term to be familiar with is "cladistics." Cladistics is a method of categorizing organisms into groups (clads) based on shared characteristics among their most recent ancestors. Cladistic classification is a tool used in phylogenetical studies.

Of course, since both cladistics and phylogeny have as their foundation the assumption that evolution is true, logically that means they cannot be used to prove evolution is true. However, the diagrams they produce are commonly used as proof of evolution.

Bird Phylogeny

The best known phylogeny of birds was done by Dr. John Ahlquist and Dr. Charles Sibly. Published in 1991, the *"Phylogeny and*

Classification of Birds" became an influential phylogeny for birds, and is now known as the Sibley–Ahlquist taxonomy.

Dr. Jon Ahlquist (Ph.D. from Yale) was a molecular biologist who specialized in molecular phylogenetics who was also an ornithologist (bird expert). In 1988 he was a co-recipient of the Daniel Giraud Elliot Medal from the U.S. National Academy of Science for his work in bird DNA. He held professorships at Ohio University, the University of Louisville (Kentucky), and several South Carolina universities. He taught a variety of subjects that include ornithology, comparative vertebrate anatomy, avian biology, molecular evolution, and systematic zoology. He was the leader in the field of bird evolution. He passed away in 2020 at the age of 75.

Dr. Ahlquist was a Christian who believed in evolution. However, in 1991 his continued study in both science and the Bible resulted in his changing his understanding of our origins from evolution to Biblical creation. He had noticed a problem in the field where he was the recognized expert... bird phylogenetics. He states:

> "The techniques used by phylogeneticists to make their 'trees' are laden with evolutionary assumptions. They simply assume that evolution is a fact and then stuff their data into their algorithms, which therefore will always produce an evolutionary result. Regardless, we all have the same data; the difference is how we interpret it.[57]"

Dr. Ahlquist was a leading expert in the field of bird evolution. He wrote the book. Then he realized it was all based on assumptions, not science, and he repudiated his past work.

This is common. When someone actually digs into the methods and processes on which the "proofs" of bird evolution are based, what they find are not scientific facts, but a foundation of unproven assumptions and circular reasoning. That is true of all evolutionary "proofs."

However, let's take the time to look at archaeopteryx in more detail in the next chapter.

---

[57] https://creation.com/jon-ahlquist

Dinosaurs Became Birds? Just Wishful Thinking

CHAPTER 17
ARCHAEOPTERYX?

Evolution should have produced billions of transitional fossils. With the many steps required to evolve from one kind of animal to another, we should be buried in transitional fossils. However, that is not the case. There are only handful of possible transitions, and most of those are disputed even within evolutionary circles. One of the most accepted transitional fossils, except among ornithologists, bird experts who know it is a true bird, is archaeopteryx. So what is archaeopteryx? A transitional fossil? A bird? Or something else?

What Dinosaur Features Does Archaeopteryx Have?

The proposition is that Archaeopteryx has a combination of dinosaur features and bird features, making it a transition from a dinosaur to a bird. What is the evidence?

#1 - Archaeopteryx has teeth. They say birds do not have teeth and dinosaurs do. Therefore, it is like a dinosaur... except there are other bird fossils that have teeth... and there are dinosaurs that don't have teeth.

#2 - Archaeopteryx has a long tail. Birds do not have long tails and dinosaurs do. So archaeopteryx is like a dinosaur... except there are other bird fossils that also have long tails.

Archaeopteryx

#3 - Archaeopteryx has claws on its wings. Birds do not have claws on their wings... well some birds do.

#4 - Birds have hollow bones. Some dinosaurs have hollow bones. They are the same! Not so fast. Hollow bones provide lightweight strength. A theropod dinosaur,[58] Majungatholus atopusi, has hollow bones. However, so do some big sauropods and pterosaurs. No one thinks birds evolved from them. When a strong, yet lightweight structure is needed, whether in a bird or a dinosaur, hollow bones are a design feature that meets the need. When a similar task needs to be accomplished, it is not unusual to see a similar solution.

Standing on its own, without a presupposition that birds evolved from dinosaurs, the evidence is weak.

What Bird Features Does Archaeopteryx Have?

It obvious that archaeopteryx has feathers. Fully developed, true flight feathers, the same design as modern flight feathers. In other words, bird feathers. In addition, the wing and tail feathers are asymmetric, just like modern birds. Modern birds have several types of feathers, and this is seen in archaeopteryx. Its feathers are differentiated into the various structures of modern feathers. Archaeopteryx looks just like a modern bird.

Archaeopteryx had perching feet, with the hallux pointing backwards, just like modern perching birds.

From the structure of the brain case we know that archaeopteryx had a bird's brain, proportionally three times larger than a dinosaur brain, and a bird's inner ear. These are important features. In birds, but not dinosaurs, the inner ear is designed to enhance auditory and spatial sensory perception, both of which are essential to flying birds.

Archaeopteryx's anatomy strongly indicates it was well adapted to flight and that it was arboreal, meaning that it spent a lot of time in trees and dense foliage.

In vertebrates, including all theropod dinosaurs, only the lower jaw moves. In birds, the upper jaw also moves, as it does in archaeopteryx.

---

[58] Birds supposedly evolved from theropod dinosaurs.

Beginner's Guide To Tracking Dinosaurs

Archaeopteryx skeletons have a pneumatized vertebrae and pelvis. This design strongly indicates that archaeopteryx had a bird's once-through breathing system.

These fundamental characteristics of birds provide strong evidence that archaeopteryx was a unique bird, not a transitional form. The evidence points to archaeopteryx being a true bird, possibly a mosaic with some unique features. It is not a transitional form of a dinosaur evolving into a bird.

But, wait! This is not the end of the story. There is another candidate. What about microraptor?

Archaeopteryx

CHAPTER 18
MICRORAPTOR

Archaeopteryx gets a lot of press, but nearly all of the experts have recognized it is not a transitional fossil. However, that is okay. There is a new dinosaur to bird evolutionary star. Microraptor!

Microraptor. A Feathered Dinosaur?

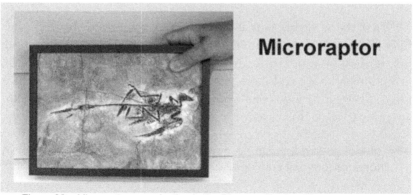

Figure 39 – Microraptor reproduction in the Dinosaur Tracker Museum

The British Natural History Museum in London proclaims microraptor is a feathered dinosaur. They describe it as a small theropod dinosaur with:

Microraptor

"...long flight feathers on all four limbs. It may have been capable of guided flight."[59]

Smithsonian Magazine (March 9, 2012) describes microraptor as an:

"...exquisitely feathered dinosaur. The small, sickle-clawed predator, which lived about 120 million years ago, was covered in well-developed plumage, including long feathers on its arms and legs."

On the other hand, quoting Dr. Elizabeth Mitchell,[60] we see there is no (zero) evidence supporting the evolution of feathers:

"Since no definitive dinosaurs with feathers have appeared in the fossil record—only dinosaurs with fuzzy-looking collagen fibers that do not qualify in any way as transitional feathers—many evolutionists seeking to explain the evolution of feathers would like to find transitional evolutionary forms. Microraptor did not help their case. Instead, these feathers appear grossly and microscopically modern both in shape and microstructure. While the researchers in this study believe their specimen is a feathered dinosaur, they have only reaffirmed the lack of evidence for feather evolution in the fossil record by shining the spotlight on the essentially modern quality of these fossil feathers—supposedly 120–130 million years old."

What she is saying is that every fossil we fine with feathers, has fully formed modern feathers. There is no sign of feather evolution. Just birds with modern feathers. So microraptor does not help the evolutionary story, and there is not much evidence that microraptor was a dinosaur. It looks like a modern bird. A 2008 NOVA program attempts to make the case for microraptor being a transition:[61]

"...it looked like it could be a missing link, with a bird's wing and a dinosaur's long tail and legs."

And then later in the program a similar statement is made:

"He's also quite sure that it was a dinosaur. Numerous details of the skeleton say so, from the long bony tail to the sickle claws on its feet."

---

[59] https://www.nhm.ac.uk/discover/dino-directory/microraptor.html
[60] Feathered Fossil: Still A Bird (March 17, 2012),
https://answersingenesis.org/dinosaurs/feathers/feathered-fossil-still-a-bird/
[61] https://www.pbs.org/wgbh/nova/evolution/four-winged-dinosaur.html

Beginner's Guide To Tracking Dinosaurs

As with archaeopteryx, it comes down to having a tail and claws. On the other hand they have to admit that, like archaeopteryx (again from the NOVA program),

> "This animal has feathers like feathers in flying birds. The wing feathers are asymmetrical, with veins wider on one side of the shaft than the other, which forms airfoil contour, like an airplane wing. Only flying birds have asymmetrical flight feathers."

So we have an animal with modern, true flight feathers. Simply having a long bony tail and sickle claws does not make a dinosaur. So what is it?

Microraptor: More Evidence

Microraptor fossils have been found with undigested meals in their stomachs. They must have been buried very quickly for that to happen.

One microraptor has a reptile in its stomach. It was eaten head first, a characteristic of birds. Another microraptor has a two-winged bird in its stomach, again eaten head first. This is some interesting evidence. Dinosaurs are not known to eat birds. A bird could easily fly away from a dinosaur. A bird in a microraptor's stomach head first indicates it could hunt, kill, and eat fully formed flying birds. That is something only other birds do.

It is starting to look like it is evolutionary doctrine; the belief that dinosaurs evolved into birds, that is driving the conclusion that microraptor is a transition from dinosaur to bird. It is wishful thinking, not science.

The body design of microraptor shows it was arboreal. It spent a lot of time in trees and dense foliage. Dinosaurs do not do that.

What about its four wings?

It has normal wings, plus feathers on its legs giving it another set of "wings." That would make flying very awkward. However, feathers on legs do not necessarily mean wings. As is common with fossils, microraptor fossils are squashed flat. The weight of the sediment on top of them tends to do that to all fossils. It is difficult to see the orientation of the leg feathers. Present-day raptors have feathers on

Microraptor

their legs that stick out straight back. They do not interfere with flying and may provide stabilization during flight.

And by the way, as you can see from the photo on page 93, microraptor was small. About the size of a present-day crow.

The preponderance of the evidence indicates microraptor was a bird. Fully a bird. A unique bird, but still a bird, not a transition. However, let's ask another question. Is it even possible for a dinosaur to evolve into a bird?

CHAPTER 19
IS DINOSAUR TO BIRD EVOLUTION EVEN POSSIBLE?

Is dinosaur to bird evolution possible? The answer is no.

One way to look at this is the fact that evolution has been scientifically proven to be impossible. We are actually devolving, getting worse and losing information, instead of evolving. This is discussed in books such as "Darwin Devolves" by Dr. Michael Behe and "Undeniable" by Dr. Douglas Axe. But, that's not the approach we will be taking. Dinosaur to bird evolution is also impossible because the changes required would kill the dinosaur[62] before it could become a bird. Here are just a couple of examples.

Lungs and Cardiovascular

This first one is definitely a dinosaur killer. Dinosaurs have bellows lungs that are similar to those of present-day crocodiles. They breathe in, and then they breathe out, similar to the way we breathe. The cardiovascular structure of theropods is designed to meet the needs of short bursts of high energy, but overall theropods are not continuously high-energy animals. They even have narrow nostrils

---

[62] www.AJ83.com/birds

Is Dinosaur To Bird Evolution Even Possible?

(low air flow) like a crocodile. On the other hand, flying is a continuous high-energy activity, and birds have a cardiovascular system designed to meet the needs of flying. To get the huge amount of oxygen they need, birds have a once-through type lung system that has five sacs. It is a system that continuously supplies oxygen, unlike our bellows in-and-out system. Why? Because that is what it takes to fly.

There is no viable step-by-step pathway to go from a bellows lung to a once-through lung. They are radically different. You cannot have half of one and half of the other. Both would be nonfunctional and the dinosaur dies. Why? If the needed structures started to develop, it still cannot be used until fully functional. The result is that these useless additions interfere with and degrade the existing respiratory system. The useless changes place such an added burden on the dinosaur that natural selection would eliminate the dinosaur (the dinosaur dies).

It is simple to say the words, "Dinosaur lungs evolved to become bird lungs." without considering the changes involved. However, from the perspective of providing the needed oxygen while the change in lung design is taking place… it cannot happen.

But wait, believers in evolution cry! What about Majungatholus atopusi. That is a dinosaur with some hollow bones. This means it has a once through air system just like a bird's. Setting aside the fact that holes in bones do not mean the dinosaur has a respiratory system like a bird, let us assume it does. That does not solve the problem. You still have to get from a bellows lung in dinosaurs in general, to a once through lung in a Majungatholus atopusi dinosaur. And that pathway leads to death.

Arm and Wing Movement

Flying not only requires a lot of energy, it requires strength to move wings. In a paper titled *"Muscle Function in Avian Flight: Achieving Power and Control"* Andrew Biewener writes:

> "The smaller supracoracoideus lies deep to the pectoralis, also originating from the keel of the sternum, and is about one-fifth of the pectoralis in mass (approx. 2% body mass). By means of its tendon,

which inserts and acts dorsally at the shoulder **as a pulley**, the supracoracoideus elevates and supinates the wing during upstroke."[63]

In other, simpler words, bird muscles use a pulley system to provide a lot of power to their wings. On the other hand, Biewener states:

"This is in contrast to terrestrial locomotion, which offers mechanisms for minimizing energy losses associated with body movement combined with elastic energy savings to reduce the skeletal muscles' work requirements."[64]

In other words, land animals (dinosaurs) have a completely different design that is optimized to minimize energy losses and reduce the stresses on the skeleton. Two very different designs to accomplish two very different purposes.

As with lungs, any change in the design results in the complete system becoming non-functional. Why? The two systems are designed in very different ways to do very different things. If a part of the system is no longer there because it evolved into something different, the overall system no longer functions. If the system for moving dinosaur arms changes a little bit -- evolution happens by small changes accumulating over long time periods -- the dinosaur loses arm function. They become less fit for survival, natural selection does its thing, and they die.

I will say it again, it is easy to say the words, "Dinosaur arms evolved to become bird wings." but the changes are so significant and destructive to the existing system that it could never happen. The dinosaur would die, and the change would never become fixed in the population.

Hip Structure

We talked about the two different types of dinosaur hips at the beginning of this book. Let us quickly review:

---

[63] Biewener AA. "Muscle Function in Avian Flight: Achieving Power and Control." Philos Trans R Soc Lond B Biol Sci., May 2011

[64] Ibid.

Is Dinosaur To Bird Evolution Even Possible?

Dinosaurs are categorized into two main groups based on their hip design. The ornithischian dinosaurs, also known as bird hipped dinosaurs, have a pubis bone that points backward. The saurischian dinosaurs, also known as lizard-hipped, have a pubis bone that points forward. Here is what is strange. Birds have a pubis bone that points to the back like ornithischian dinosaurs, yet it is thought that birds evolved from saurischian (theropod) dinosaurs. That means that in the evolutionary process the publis bone had to swing around from the front, to point to the back, as well as change its structural design. Seems a little far-fetched.

The pubis bone has several functions. Two of its major functions are to stabilize the pelvic girdle and serve as an attachment point for muscles. It is an integral part of the body.

The need to reorient the pubis bone has caused quite a discussion among evolutionists. For example, did a rear pointing pubis evolve twice? Once in dinosaurs and separately in birds? However, the biggest question is how could a dinosaur survive such a change?

The pubis cannot just swing around. And even if a new, forward facing pubis bone grew, how would evolution "know" that the muscle attachments needed to change. Evolution is blind. It cannot "see" what will be needed and then produce it. On top of this, we run into the same problems as before. As small changes are occurring to the pubis, it no longer serves the purpose for which it was designed. The dinosaur loses the functions provided by the pubis, is less fit to survive, and dies.

These are just three examples. There are others, such as the need to change the design of the brain, the skull, and the inner ear. From a practical view, changing a dinosaur into a bird will not work. The changes will harm the animal, and natural selection will select it to die.

CHAPTER 20
FACT CHECK: EVOLUTION

Human and Chimp DNA is 98% Similar

Fact Check: NOT TRUE

Even the Journal Science called this a myth way back in 2007. Yet it is still being presented as a fact.

In 1975 human and chimpanzee DNA was compared. The result? They were 98.5% similar! (This was rounded up to 99% in most cases.) Proclaim it to the world! It has been proven! Humans and chimpanzees are related. Evolution is true!

However, there is more to the story.

In those initial tests, they did not compare the entire DNA of chimpanzees and humans. They selectively used portions of human and chimpanzee DNA that were already known to be similar. In 1998, for the first time, the full genome of both chimpanzees and humans was compared. The result? About an 85% similarity. That means there is a huge difference. Millions of differences. Even if evolution is true, 85% is too great of a gap to overcome in the six millions years (based on evolution) since the human and chimpanzee lines diverged. In fact, even 1%, which represents 30,000,000 changes to the DNA, is too great of a gap.

Fact Check: Evolution

"Sequence similarity does not mean functional equivalence nor does it prove common ancestry."[65]

"While humans display some distinct similarities to apes, in the most important aspects we are utterly unique. Only humans can do science, sequence their own genome, reason, engineer cities, visit the moon, write books/programs/poetry/music, or show agape love. We clearly have dominion over the earth. Biblically, only man is a moral being with a soul, capable of communion with God. In all of these respects we are incredibly unique."[66]

The human-chimpanzee myth is BUSTED! But don't expected it to go away. Myths about evolution continue to be used to "prove" evolution.

Antibiotic Resistance Shows Evolution in Action

Fact Check: NOT TRUE

To understand this one we need to understand evolution. Evolution is commonly defined simply as change. However, what is not included in this definition is the quality of the change. What is the overall result of the change? Is it overall doing good... or is it harmful?

An old car left in a field is rusting away. It is changing. Is it getting better? No. There can be change that brings improvement and change that destroys. Moreover, there can be changes that do nothing. These are called neutral changes.

What is observed in living organisms is that random mutations are harmful[67]. These mutations, which are supposedly the source of the change that drives evolution, are in fact devolutionary. They are harmful, degrading our fitness. What is interesting is that those harmful changes can have short term benefits. Dr. Michael Behe (a biochemist) writes in his book "Darwin Devolves:"

---

[65] Christopher Rupe and Dr. John Sanford, "Contested Bones", FMS Publications, (2019) page 139
[66] Ibid page 347
[67] "It is thought that beneficial mutations may be so rare that their rarity cannot be measured." Ibid page 311

Beginner's Guide To Tracking Dinosaurs

"Now, several decades into the 21st century, ever more sophisticated studies demonstrate that, ironically, random mutation and natural selection are in fact fiercely devolutionary. It turns out that mutation easily breaks or degrades genes, which counterintuitively, can sometimes help an organism to survive."[68]

This describes what is happening when a bacteria becomes resistant to an antibiotic. The bacteria has degraded. For example, it may have lost the ability to metabolize the antibiotic. As a result, the antibiotic no longer kills it. Alternatively, it may have lost the ability to move the antibiotic across the cell membrane. The antibiotic can no longer get into the cell to kill it. However, in every case the bacteria has lost an ability. It has degraded, and is actually overall weaker than it was before, even though it is now resistant to the antibiotic.

The antibiotic resistance myth is BUSTED! However, do not expected it to go away. Myths about evolution continue to be used to "prove" evolution. It does not matter if they are actually true or not.

Speciation - Evolution Happening Right before Our Eyes

Fact Check: NOT TRUE

With this claim, we are encountering a propaganda technique known as equivocation. What this means is that the definition of a word is changed, without your knowing it. The word is "evolution."

It starts with evolution being defined as "change." Sometimes they expand it a little and say evolution is "change over time." Sometimes they may make it more complicated, "change in the genome." However it is said, it still simply means change.

Based on that definition evolution is true. Look at the different rabbits in figure 40. We see change... they look different. The ears are different. Their fur is different. We see different species of rabbits. It is evolution in action! Proof evolution is true! You can see it for yourself!

Do you see how the definition of evolution changed?

---

[68] Michael Behe, "Darwin Devolves," HarperOne, 2019, page 10

Fact Check: Evolution

When you hear the word "evolution" what comes to mind? An ape-like creature evolving to become a human. A dinosaur evolving to become a bird. You think of something evolving to become something completely different. That is the assumed definition of the word "evolution." One kind of life becoming something totally different. What is given as proof evolution happens? Rabbits producing more rabbits is defined as evolution, and thus evolution is proven true.

Figure 40 – There are many breeds and species of rabbits, however, they are all still... rabbits.

Yes, there are many species of rabbits. However, what are they? Rabbits. There are many species of cats. However, what are they all? Cats. They may be different sizes, and colors, and have different fur... but they are all still cats. That there are different species of rabbits or cats, does not provide any proof that a rabbit can evolve to become a cat, or a cat to become a rabbit. That would be evolution. What speciation proves is that evolution never happens. Why? Because cats always make more cats, no matter which species of cat they are. And rabbits ALWAYS make more rabbits (and a lot of them), no matter which species of rabbit they are.

The idea that speciation proves evolution is BUSTED! It is a myth. However, do not expected it to go away. Myths about evolution continue to be used to "prove" evolution. It does not matter if they are actually true or not, as long as they convince people to believe in evolution.

CHAPTER 21
HUMAN EVOLUTION MYTHS

Defining Human Evolution

The encyclopedia Britannica defines "human evolution" this way:

> "The process by which human beings developed on Earth from now-extinct primates. The only extant members of the human tribe, Hominini, belong to the species Homo sapiens. The exact nature of the evolutionary relationships between modern humans and their ancestors remains the subject of debate."[69]

Note that the last sentence of the definition recognizes that there are no evolutionary links between modern humans and extinct primates, or what we would simply call apes. However, that is not why I quoted this definition.

To make this definition more accurate, the word "non-human" needs to be added to the first sentence. The definition will then say, *"The process by which human beings developed on Earth from now-extinct non-human primates."*

Now we have a more precise first sentence that excludes God and Biblical creation, which ultimately is the purpose of evolution. Let's take the next step and see if there is any evidence supporting this definition.

---

[69] https://www.britannica.com/science/human-evolution.

Human Evolution Myths

Is There Evidence Human Beings Developed from Now-Extinct Non-human Primates?

The claim is that there is abundant evidence. The *BBC Earth* web page provides a good summary:

> "For scientists, evolution is a fact. We know that life evolved with the same certainty that we know the Earth is roughly spherical, that gravity keeps us on it, and that wasps at a picnic are annoying... Why are biologists so certain about this? What is the evidence? The short answer is that there is so much it's hard to know where to start."[70]

If this is true, there must be a lot of SOLID, FACTUAL evidence evolution happened. On the other hand, does the evidence instead point to two separate and distinct groups, humans and non-humans, both having been designed and created by God? (No evolution.) Let's see what proof the BBC has.

The BBC Starts With Equivocation

The BBC starts by defining and describing evolution:

> "Breeders work just like Darwin imagined evolution worked. Suppose you want to breed chickens that lay more eggs. First, you must find those hens that lay more eggs than the others. Then you must hatch their eggs, and ensure that the resulting chicks reproduce. These chicks should also lay more eggs. If you repeat the process with each generation, eventually you'll have hens that lay far more eggs than wild chickens do."

> "'That's what evolution is,' says Steve Jones of University College London in the UK. 'It's a series of mistakes that build up.'"[71]

That is their definition, and it is pure equivocation. What is described here is not evolution. At best, the BBC definition describes speciation, which everyone accepts as happening. This is how evolution is "proven," by defining it as something it is not. That is not proof. That is called sleight of hand, deception, trickery. Yes, you will

---

[70] http://www.bbc.com/earth/story/20150803-how-do-we-know-evolution-is-real
[71] Ibid.

have chickens that lay more eggs (there is a limit, however), but they will still be chickens. When the chicken eggs hatch there will always be a chicken inside. That is a fact of observational and repeatable science.

When a definition like the BBC definition is used, it is easy to see why a claim of lots of evidence supporting evolution can be made. Its evidence that supports something we all agree happens, but it does not actually address evolution... all life coming from non-life, and humans developing from non-human primates.

Maybe We're Going to Get an Answer

The BBC page then talks about the different forms of life we see in the fossil record. They ask:

"How do we really know that one species evolved into another?"

Good question! It is not the right question[72], but it is still a good question. Here is their answer:

"The fossil record is only so much help here, because it is incomplete. If you look at most fossil records, what you actually see is one form that lasts quite a long time and then the next bunch of fossils that you've got is quite different from what you had before,'" says Jones.[73]"

Sounds like they are describing Biblical creation and a global flood that created fossils based on how long animals could avoid being buried by sediment. They have stated the truth of what the fossil record shows. There is no solid evidence supporting evolution in the fossil record. So they switch from talking about fossils to talking about species.

"It is also possible to observe the evolution of a new species as it happens. In 1981, a single medium ground finch arrived on an island called Daphne Major. He was unusually large and sang a somewhat different song to the local birds. He managed to breed,

---

[72] "Evolution" is not one species "evolving" into another species. It is one kind of life changing to become a different kind of life.
[73] Ibid.

and his offspring inherited his unusual traits. After a few generations, they were reproductively isolated: they looked different from the other birds, and sang different songs, so could only breed among themselves. This little group of birds had formed a new species: they had "speciated".

They are back to speciation as a proof of evolution. The above started with a finch and ended with a finch. It was a finch with some different characteristics, but it was still a finch. For evolution to be seen the finch must become something other than a finch. We are back to equivocation, not a proof of evolution.

For the next example the article brings up an ongoing experiment conducted by Richard Lenski.[74] He has been culturing e-coli bacteria in a stressful environment since 1988. They are in conditions favoring mutation. However, what are they today? Still e-coli. This experiment does not show evolution. It is a grand demonstration that evolution does not happen, even under the most favorable of circumstances. After more than 74,000 generations, and under environmental pressure to mutate, the result is... e-coli are still e-coli.

The following describes what has been learned from the ongoing Lenski experiment:

> "In a reductive biological situation, a population is put under very special conditions that favor the purging of functional information that is non-essential for the moment (eg, the LTEE of Lenski et al.). These loss-of-function mutations appear to be beneficial because organisms can temporarily grow faster. However, such reductive mutations are actually destroying information and narrowing the organism's ecological range."[75]

What this quote is saying is that, this experiment demonstrates that when organisms are put in a stressful environment designed to eliminate the need for certain features, they will lose those features and be better suited for the specialized environment in which those features are of no use. That is not evolution. The e-coli have experienced reductive mutations; have lost capabilities they originally had; and have overall become less fit to survive. The have gone downhill... they have not evolved, they have de-evolved.

---

[74] See: http://www.bbc.com/earth/story/20150803-how-do-we-know-evolution-is-real

[75] Christopher Rupe and Dr. John Sanford, "Contested Bones", FMS Publications, (2019) page 312

CHAPTER 22
DEFINING EVOLUTION

This may be the most important topic we discuss in this book. The following is a fundamental principle: Whoever controls the definition of words, controls the conversation and your thoughts.

No, there is no more to the above sentence. The person, group, government, or... whoever controls the definition of words, will be the ones who are in control of not just the conversation, but your mind and actions. We see that in politics. We see it in religious cults.

This is what evolution is all about. Evolution is not about science. It has everything to do with controlling the way you think about God, life and yourself. It starts with the definition of the word "evolution."

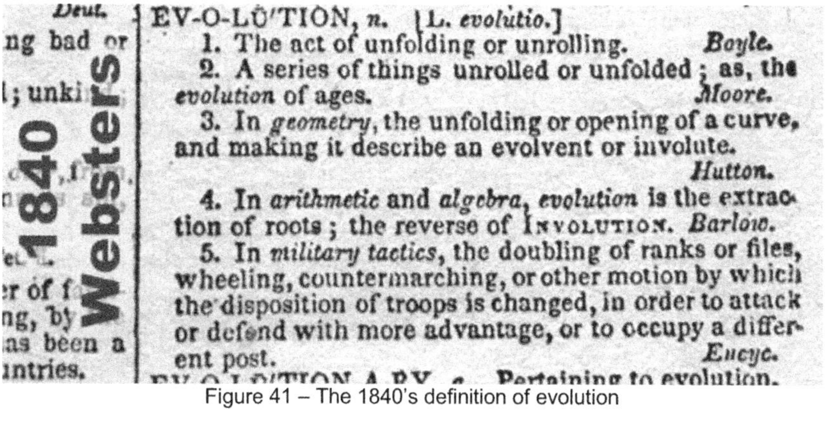

EV-O-LŨ'TION, n. [L. evolutio.]
1. The act of unfolding or unrolling. *Boyle.*
2. A series of things unrolled or unfolded; as, the evolution of ages. *Moore.*
3. In *geometry*, the unfolding or opening of a curve, and making it describe an evolvent or involute. *Hutton.*
4. In *arithmetic* and *algebra*, evolution is the extraction of roots; the reverse of INVOLUTION. *Barlow.*
5. In *military tactics*, the doubling of ranks or files, wheeling, countermarching, or other motion by which the disposition of troops is changed, in order to attack or defend with more advantage, or to occupy a different post. *Encyc.*

Figure 41 – The 1840's definition of evolution

Figure 41 shows the definition of the word evolution in Webster's 1840 dictionary. Darwin would not publish *"On the Origin of Species by Means of Natural Selection or the Preservation of Favoured Races in the Struggle For Life"* until 1859.

100 years later in the 1942 Webster's Dictionary (figure 42) the definition has changed to include Darwinian evolution:

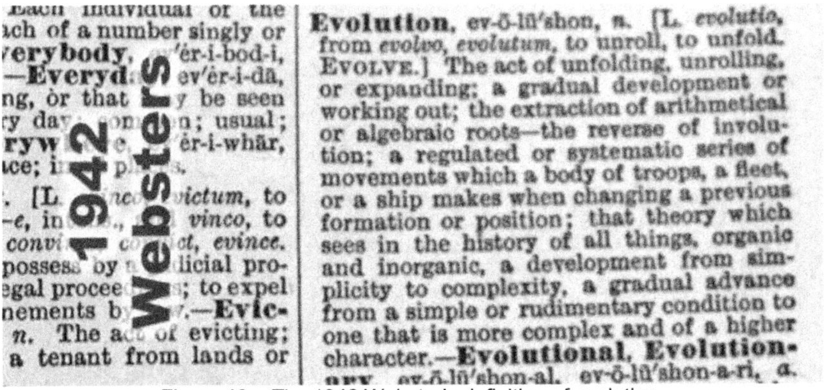

Evolution, ev-ō-lū'shon, *n.* [L. *evolutio*, from *evolvo*, *evolutum*, to unroll, to unfold. EVOLVE.] The act of unfolding, unrolling, or expanding; a gradual development or working out; the extraction of arithmetical or algebraic roots—the reverse of involution; a regulated or systematic series of movements which a body of troops, a fleet, or a ship makes when changing a previous formation or position; that theory which sees in the history of all things, organic and inorganic, a development from simplicity to complexity, a gradual advance from a simple or rudimentary condition to one that is more complex and of a higher character.—**Evolutional**, **Evolutionary**, ev-ō-lū'shon-al, ev-ō-lū'shon-a-ri, *a.*

Figure 42 – The 1942 Webster's definition of evolution.

> "That theory which sees in the history of all things, organic and inorganic, a development from simplicity to complexity, a gradual advance from a simple or rudimentary condition to one that is more complex and of a higher character."

This definition is not bad. It is a fairly accurate representation of what most people bring to mind when they hear the word "evolution." Life developing from simplicity to complexity. This definition is reasonably good even for today. However, there was a problem. By the late 1960's it was obvious that observations did not support this definition.

Today the **Merriam-Webster** definition is:

> "Descent with modification from preexisting species: cumulative inherited change in a population of organisms through time leading to the appearance of new forms the process by which new species or populations of living things develop from preexisting forms through successive generations."

There is a secondary definition:

Beginner's Guide To Tracking Dinosaurs

"The scientific theory explaining the appearance of new species and varieties through the action of various biological mechanisms (such as natural selection, genetic mutation or drift, and hybridization)."

What we have in the above, is a more complex definition that applies to "species." However, as a definition of the word "evolution" this is a straight out lie. Properly defining "evolution" using the framework of the above definition, requires the word "species" to be replaced by "domain."[76] That truly describes evolution. Evolution requires the ability to change a life form in one domain so that it becomes a life form in a new domain. That is far, far away from a change at the species level.

Why the change?

Because in the 1940's we began to understand the complexity of the cell and genetics. Over the next couple of decades it became apparent that the 1942 definition was not supported by the evidence. That meant the goalposts needed to be moved. In this case it was like moving the evolution goalpost to the 50 yard line and still calling it NFL football.

Control the Definition - You Control Minds

Before you can prove whether a statement is true, you must first clearly define what you are asserting. Here is a painfully simple example. You say, "Call me a taxi, please." I respond, "You're a taxi!" We defined the word "call" differently. In this simple example, it is easy to see how the definition of the word "call" changed. This is what happens with the word "evolution," but in a more complex way.

I will say it again, before anyone attempts to prove something as being either true or false, they must accurately define what that something is. In other words, to prove evolution true, we must be clear on what the word "evolution" means. If I am thinking the 1942 definition and you are thinking the 2021 definition, you can pronounce

---

[76] This does not preclude evolutionary changes at the phylum, order, genus, or even species level. However, for evolution to be true it must be capable of evolving an organism in one genus, class, kingdom or domain to become an organism in a different genus, class, kingdom or domain. In other words, it has to include single cell life evolving to become complex human life, and all the changes in between. (It also has to include the formation of proteins from non-living matter, before there was life.)

Defining Evolution

evolution proven true and be correct in your mind and wrong in my mind. So we must agree on a definition of the word "evolution" before we can talk about truth.

In attempt to clarify the evolution discussion the noted British zoologist and physiologist Dr. Gerald Kerkut, distinguishes between the two major ways the word evolution is used:

> "There is a theory which states that many living animals can be observed over the course of time to undergo changes so that new species are formed. This can be called the 'Special Theory of Evolution' and can be demonstrated in certain cases by experiments. On the other hand there is the theory that all the living forms in the world have arisen from a single source which itself came from an inorganic form. This theory can be called the 'General Theory of Evolution.' and the evidence that supports it is not sufficiently strong to allow us to consider it as anything more than a working hypothesis.[77]"

To summarize in as brief a form as possible: the Special Theory of Evolution (STE) is defined as speciation, the General Theory of Evolution (GTE) as all life originating from a common ancestor. When someone is claiming there is solid proof that evolution is true, the definition of "evolution" that comes to mind is the GTE definition, all life coming from a common ancestor. That is what Darwin claimed was true. HOWEVER, what they are actually talking about today is the STE definition. There is abundant proof speciation happens. However, that is not evolution as we commonly think of it.

What are they doing? They are claiming that speciation, and all life coming from a common ancestor, are equivalent. However, they have not proven that. They have not presented any evidence these two are equivalent. All they have done is show speciation happens, and then declared, with no evidence; speciation is equivalent to all life having a common ancestor. That is why it is called equivocation and it is a very powerful propaganda technique, especially when you do not know it is being used against you.

Proving that the Special Theory of Evolution is true, does not prove that the General Theory of Evolution is true. By the way, bring this up with an evolution evangelist, and they will reject the Kerkut

---

[77] Kerkut, G.A., "Implications of Evolution," Pergamon, Oxford, UK, (1960) page 157, ia600409.us.archive.org/23/items/implicationsofev00kerk/implicationsofev00kerk.pdf

Beginner's Guide To Tracking Dinosaurs

definitions. They know that, if they accept that definition, they have lost the argument. They know that when they can no longer impose a false definition, they have lost the debate.

Another way to look at it is that in presenting a proof, ALL of the steps must be proven true. In high school algebra, leaving out one step, even if it is obvious, means it is an invalid proof. Even if you have the right answer, the teacher will mark it wrong. Evolution evangelists never prove that speciation results in all life arising from a common ancestor... becoming more complex in the process -- explaining the observed fact that we are much more complex than a bacteria, for example. They do not provide that proof, because they cannot provide that proof.

Defining Evolution

CHAPTER 23
BBC GETS IT WRONG

BBC Uses A "Proof" That Has Been Proven False

When it comes to proving that evolution happened, at times the proofs can be out of date. In other words, claims that are no longer valid continue to be used to prove evolution happened. The next part of the BBC web page provides an example. Here is what they say:

> "Over the last century scientists have catalogued the genes from different species. It turns out that all living things store information in their DNA in the same way: they all use the same 'genetic code'.
>
> "What's more, organisms also share many genes. Thousands of genes found in human DNA may also be found in the DNA of other creatures, including plants and even bacteria.
>
> "These two facts imply that all modern life has descended from a single common ancestor, the 'last universal ancestor', which lived billions of years ago.
>
> "By comparing how many genes organisms share, we can figure out how they are related. For instance, humans share more genes with apes like chimps and gorillas than other animals, as much as 96%. That suggests they are our closest relatives.[78]"

---

[78] http://www.bbc.com/earth/story/20150803-how-do-we-know-evolution-is-real

BBC Gets It Wrong

CLAIM #1 - All living things use DNA in the same way to store information: and this means all living things originated from a common ancestor. That is a huge leap of blind faith. Might it be that DNA is the best, most highly optimized method for storing genetic information, and a common designer would create such an information storage system and then use it throughout all that He creates?

CLAIM #2 - The same genes used in human DNA are found in other living things: and this means all living things originated from a common ancestor. The BBC assumes there is no other explanation.

On the other hand, might it be that instead of a common ancestor, living things, since they are all carbon-based, do similar things? DNA provides the instructions for making proteins. Might it be possible (actually it is a fact) that all living things use many of the same proteins?

Also, a critically important fact the BBC ignores is that, there is more to genetics than just DNA sequences. The same gene can perform different functions.

> "We are beginning to see that there are profound ape/human differences that transcend DNA sequences. This includes many epigenetic systems such as differential nucleosome formation, 3-D DNA structure, DNA methylation, transcription, RNA splicing, RNA editing, protein translation, and protein glycosylation."[79]

What he is saying is that there is more to DNA than just comparing DNA sequences. For example, there are multiple ways in which the same DNA sequence can produce different results. That means counting similar DNA sequences is meaningless. It tells us nothing about the actual differences between two organisms. Genetics and DNA information storage is not as simple and linear as reading a book. Simply counting DNA sequences and declaring that two organism are similar is scientifically absurd.[80]

---

[79] Christopher Rupe and Dr. John Sanford, "Contested Bones", FMS Publications, (2019) page 311

[80] We are just starting to grasp how complex DNA is. It has been described as operating in four dimensions. For example. DNA produces proteins. However, a protein can be folded in different ways to perform different functions. Just because a certain gene may produce a certain protein, that does not mean that protein functions the same

Beginner's Guide To Tracking Dinosaurs

Chimp and Human DNA are 96% Similar?

The BBC claims that chimpanzee and human DNA is 96% similar. The 96% number comes from a 2005 issue of the Journal Nature (a British publication). That 4% represents 120,000,000 DNA base pair differences. That is a big number.

Let's set aside what we just discussed on the previous page and look at this from another viewpoint. A good question to start with is; what is being compared? These studies do not look at the entire genome, meaning they pick only certain portions of chimpanzee DNA to be compared with certain portions of human DNA. Portions already known to be similar. What are the results you would expect from that? Of course they are going to appear to be similar.

In 2018 Dr. Jeffrey Tomkins (a geneticist) was interviewed by Brian Thomas[81]. In that interview Dr. Tomkins makes the point that many of the DNA databases used for doing DNA comparisons are contaminated with human DNA. This skews the results making chimpanzee DNA seem more human-like. In addition, the chimpanzee genome is assembled using the human genome as a scaffold... building in similarities that actually do not exist. What Dr. Tomkins' research is showing is that, doing a true uncontaminated comparison, there is no more than an 85% similarity between chimpanzee and human DNA. Based on DNA there is no feasible way humans and chimpanzees could have evolved from a common ancestor.

Why do they use human DNA to scaffold chimpanzee DNA? Because it is "known" that chimpanzees and humans have a common ancestor, so it makes sense to use human DNA to scaffold the assembly of chimpanzee DNA. Then when the results show they are similar, evolution is proven true... through circular reasoning once again.

Here is an interesting fact. Chimpanzee DNA is 12% larger than human DNA. That means that, if the rest of the chimpanzee DNA is an exact duplicate of human DNA, there is a minimum of a 12% difference. In addition, there are about 42 million bases present in humans that are mot found in chimpanzees and about 40 million found in chimpanzees that are not found in humans. These are also

---

way. Also, a protein function may change based on other proteins that are present. So DNA similarity is only a small part of the overall story of how DNA functions.

[81] https://www.icr.org/article/human-chimp-dna-comparison

not taken into account in the comparison studies. So the difference, before any DNA comparison starts, is even greater.

It is starting to look like humans and chimpanzees are not genetically similar at all… no matter how you look at it. Once you get the complete story, it is obvious humans and chimpanzees are not related.

Visually chimpanzees look like us more than any other animal. However, there is more to it. In an article titled *"Decoding the Dogma of DNA Similarity"* Daniel Anderson writes:

> "However, there are some extremely significant differences between chimps and humans. Our skeletal anatomy, though bearing some similarity, is very different. Our skulls, necks, spines, limb proportions, pelvis, hands, and feet provide some of the most glaring differences. Our soft tissue arrangements also create a stark contrast in external appearance (e.g., everted lips, nasal bridge, whites of eyes). Some of our protein expression and brain biochemistry are radically different as well.
>
> "Perhaps the most profound differences come in areas such as language, art, music, mathematics, technology, philosophy, animal husbandry, agriculture, and a moral and spiritual capacity. This is powerful confirmation of the Genesis account in which human beings alone are created in the image of God. We are not highly evolved apes."[82]

Are Random Mutations Beneficial? No!

For evolution to work, mutations must be beneficial. They must make changes to the genome that result in an increase in the organism's complexity. That requires an increase in the information content of DNA. Is this what is observed? No. What is observed is that, although a random mutation might result in a short-term benefit, they result in damage and a loss of information in the genome (DNA).

> "I was therefore shocked to discover in recent reports on the human genome that beneficial mutations have not been found. Only 'deleterious' and 'functional' mutations have been documented... If we truly were evolving in the neo-Darwinian manner then among these millions of mutations we should be carrying at least some 'beneficial

---

[82] https://tinyurl.com/y336jwva

associated' mutations. None has been found. It would be REALLY BIG NEWS! Our genomes are accumulating deleterious mutations, not 'beneficial' ones, and they are losing DNA faster than they are gaining it." - Alexander Williams (botanist)[83]

"Living organisms are phenomenally complex, mutations mainly damage information, and adaptations that may be advantageous in a particular special environment (e.g. the presence of a particular disease) are still likely to be disadvantageous generally." - Andrew Lamb (Journal of Creation 20(1):15 April 2006)[84]

"The amazing but in retrospect unsurprising fact established by the diligent work of many investigators in laboratory evolution over decades in that the great majority of even beneficial positively selected mutations damage an organism's genetic information--either degrading or outright destroying functional coded elements. – Michael Behe (biochemist)[85]

Note: Not all mutations cause damage, only random mutations. There are also programmed mutations. Life is designed to adapt through the use of mutations that are programmed into our genome. Our environmental circumstances can trigger preprogrammed mutations that help us adapt to the new circumstances. This can result in a perceived increase in information. However, the information for these mutations was already built into the DNA. So nothing new is created.

How can we identify a preprogrammed mutation? In experiments done with mice it was noticed that when placed in certain stressful conditions, mice DNA would mutate so as to adapt the mice to the new conditions. This happened quickly, within a few generations. And it always happened in the same way. In the same conditions, the exact same mutation would happen every time, in every mouse lineage. This is impossible for random mutations to accomplish. Geneticists realized they had discovered preprogrammed mutations.

---

[83] https://creation.com/beneficial-mutations-real-or-imaginary-part-1

[84] https://creation.com/ccr5delta32-a-very-beneficial-mutation

[85] Michael Behe, (biochemist) Darwin Devolves, page 183, emphasis in the original

BBC Gets It Wrong

Random Mutations Mean Devolution Not Evolution

It is common sense, something everyone knows, random mutations are harmful, and they cause damage. They do not cause life to improve or gain new capabilities or functions.

This fact is obvious, except, something happens to our thinking when we are talking about evolution. For example, if random mutations provided benefits, helping us to evolve and become better, wouldn't we seek ways to cause random mutations in ourselves? We don't do that! We know mutations are harmful. We wear a lead apron when the dentist takes X-rays. We know too much sun can cause skin cancer (mutations in the skin). A nuclear power plant accident is a major catastrophe. We know random mutations are harmful.

Although even us common people know random mutation are harmful, we believe evolution evangelists when they tell us random mutations resulted in all life evolving from a single cell organism over millions of years... millions of years of harmful mutations! That is not common sense.

Random Mutations Mean Devolution NOT Evolution

Scientist have been studying genetic mutations for a long time. What they have noticed is that random mutations are harmful or at best neutral. Although the neutral ones do not result in any apparent physical harm, they still degrade the DNA, so they should also be categorized as harmful.

This does not mean these harmful mutations cannot provide a benefit. Sickle-cell anemia is a random mutation that damages hemoglobin. The hemoglobin becomes less able to carry oxygen and overall the person is degraded. For example, people with sickle cell anemia are more susceptible to infection, fatigue, episodes of pain, and vision problems. However, in malaria infested areas sickle cell anemia provides a major benefit, immunity to malaria. Yes, there can be a benefit from a degradation of the genome. Overall fitness is sacrificed in favor of a limited benefit.

Since we know random mutations are harmful, why does anyone think life can evolve from a single cell organism to the complexity of humanity? It is obviously impossible, no matter how many millions of years go by. However, evolution is not about science, or observed facts, or logic, or even common sense. Evolution is all about providing a way to deny God, while pretending to be rational and logical. Evolution is not about science, it is about people making themselves feel good, while they reject God.[86]

> *"He who believes in Him is not judged; he who does not believe has been judged already, because he has not believed in the name of the only begotten Son of God. This is the judgment,* **that the Light has come into the world, and men loved the darkness rather than the Light, for their deeds were evil.** *For everyone who does evil hates the Light, and does not come to the Light for fear that his deeds will be exposed. But he who practices the truth comes to the Light, so that his deeds may be manifested as having been wrought in God."* - John 3:18-21

The Experts Speak

"Several lines of experimental evidence show that novel functional genes and proteins cannot be formed de novo by chance processes... there are narrow limits to the changes that random processes can achieve. They can never convert one gene to a basically different gene, one protein structure to a different structure, nor one microorganism to a different one. Thus evolution is a story without a mechanism." – Dr. Matti Leisola [87]

"As Darwin himself knew, there are three very general ways in which an organism can adapt: (1) it can gain a new ability; (2) it can lose an old one; or (3) it can tweak or modify something it already has... In any case, it will never have greater genetic wealth that what it inherited. That, at least, is the picture painted by the very best, most sophisticated evolutionary experiments the biological revolution has produced to date." – Dr. Michael Behe [88]

---

[86] Unfortunately, some Christians are swept up in the evolution evangelist's rhetoric and false science, and they trust Darwin and evolution to be true. That does not mean they are not true Christians, but it presents problems for them in understanding scripture. I recommend the book "Theistic Evolution" edited by Moreland, Meyer, Shaw, Gauger and Grudem. It addresses all aspects of theistic evolution, demonstrating it is impossible from a scientific, philosophical and Biblical perspective.

[87] Dr. Matti Leisola (enzyme bioengineer), "Evolution: A Story Without a Mechanism," Theistic Evolution, 2017, page 140

[88] - Dr. Michael Behe, "Darwin Devolves", 2019, pages 179 and 197

"Virtually all the "beneficial mutations" known are only equivocally beneficial, not unequivocally beneficial. In bacteria, several mutations in cell wall proteins may deform the proteins enough so that antibiotics cannot bind to the mutant bacteria. This creates bacterial resistance to that antibiotic. Does this support evolutionary genetic theory? No, since the mutant bacteria do not survive as well in the wild as the native (non-mutant) bacteria." – Dr. Barry Maddox [89]

"The majority of mutations are "neutral mutations" that do not cause any detectable change in the phenotype or body of the animal. These mutations can only be detected by DNA sequencing and are not candidates for evolutionary processes at all. Since there is no phenotypic change, natural selection cannot even remotely select for them. And they are not totally neutral, but are rather subtly deleterious because they degrade the genetic code" – Dr. Barry Maddox [90]

---

[89] Dr. Barry Maddox, "Mutations: The Raw Material For Evolution?[89], 2007
[90] Ibid

CHAPTER 24
BBC'S PROOF OF HUMAN EVOLUTION

The BBC's Proof of Human Evolution

Let's continue looking at the BBC's web page promoting evolution. We will quote the entire next section from their web page:

"The fossil record shows a gradual change from ape-like animals walking on all fours to bipedal creatures that gradually developed bigger brains.

"The first humans to leave Africa interbred with other hominin species, such as the Neanderthals. As a result, people of European and Asian descent carry Neanderthal genes in their DNA, but people of African descent don't.

"For instance, in the 1950s a British doctor called Anthony Allison was studying a genetic disorder called sickle-cell anemia, which is common in some African populations. People with the disorder have misshapen red blood cells, which don't carry oxygen around the body as well as they might.

"For those people, it was worth carrying the sickle-cell mutation.

"Allison discovered that the east African populations were divided into groups of lowland-dwelling people, who were prone to the disease, and people who lived in the highlands, who were not.

BBC's Proof of Human Evolution

"It turned out that people carrying the sickle-cell trait got an unexpected benefit. It protected them from malaria, which was only really a threat in the lowlands. For those people, it was worth carrying the sickle-cell mutation, even if their children might be anaemic.

"By contrast, people living in highland areas were not at risk from malaria. That meant there was no advantage to carrying the sickle-cell trait, so its otherwise-harmful nature had meant it disappeared.

"Of course, there are all sorts of questions about evolution that we still haven't answered.

"Stringer offers a simple one: what was the genetic change that allowed humans to walk upright, and why was that mutation so successful? Right now we don't know, but with more fossils and better genetics, we might someday.

"What we do know is that evolution is a fact of nature. It is the basis for life on Earth as we know it.[91]

It looks like they claim three "proofs" human evolution happened:

- (1) The fossil record
- (2) Mutations provided immunity to malaria
- (3) A declaration: evolution is a fact of nature

The Fossil Record

On page 107 I quoted the BBC article as saying the fossil record does not support evolution. However, the very next statement the BBC makes contradicts what they just said:

"But as we have dug up more and more remains, a wealth of "transitional fossils" has been discovered. These "missing links" are halfway houses between familiar species."

I have had people say to me, "Look at the skulls. You can see it right there. Transitional fossils. Humans evolved." However, when

---

[91] http://www.bbc.com/earth/story/20150803-how-do-we-know-evolution-is-real

you look at the skulls, what are you seeing? Humans or apes. No transitions. All of the links are missing.

Did you catch what the BBC said in their second paragraph on page 123? Humans and Neanderthals interbred. The most basic definition of a species is that, if they can interbreed, they are the same species.[92] Neanderthals and humans are the same species. Fully human. Older artist renditions depict Neanderthals as brutish savages. We now know that if you dressed a Neanderthal in the clothes you are now wearing, no one would think of them as other than a present-day, modern human.

It is the same with the others. Homo habilis, Homo rudolfensis, Homo erectus, they are all within the range of normal variation in today's human population. Why are they classified as links in human evolution? Because believers in evolution need "evolutionary" links.

> "Homo erectus, 'is he a missing link? The answer must be no. Not as a being who stood halfway between the apes and modern humans--the skeleton is too human-like for that." - John Reader [93]

> "This is strong evidence that the bones commonly referred to as Homo erectus are fully human individuals who suffered from various pathologies associated with such things as inbreeding, mutation, teratogens (developmental abnormalities), etc." – Christopher Rupe and Dr. John Sanford [94]

A second issue is that fossils of supposed ape-like human ancestors are not found in isolation. Most were discovered mixed with other fossils. Pigs, fish, apes, fully human bones and fossils of other animals, all mixed together. As a result scientists can pick and choose which pieces to bring together to create an "ape-man" transitional fossil. They can pick some human bones, some ape bones and voila! An ape to human transition.

> "Habilis is a 'wastebasket taxon'--a commixture of Australopithecus and Homo bones. Habilis failed to fill the 'vast gulf' that separates australopith and man. Habilis can now be added to the growling list

---

[92] Biology Dictionary - https://biologydictionary.net/species/
[93] - John Reader, "Missing Links," Oxford University Press, (2011) page 146
[94] Christoher Rupe and Dr. John Sanford, "Contested Bones," (2019) page 77

of falsely claimed 'ape-men." – Christopher Rupe and Dr. John Sanford [95]

"Could the Lucy skeleton contain bones that do not belong to the same individual, or more importantly, the same species? This is not unreasonable. Lucy's skeleton was found in a mixed bone bed consisting of all types of African fauna, including primates such as monkeys and baboons." – Christopher Rupe and Dr. John Sanford [96]

[Note: one of Lucy's vertebrae segments has been found to be from a baboon.]

But what about the age of the fossils? Doesn't dating of the fossils show an evolutionary sequence?

"Evolution is always assumed and then imposed upon the evidence. Dating the fossils does not help. It is also common for evolutionists to use various dating methods, and then choose one that falls within or close to their expected evolutionary age for the fossil. For example, in the case of Homo naledi, the bones were initially given a date of 1.8 Ma ('millions of years ago') before testing was done. It was soon after re-dated it at 912 ka ('thousands of years ago') after a phylogenetic study. A couple of months later, it was tested and re-dated again at 236 ka to 414 ka. And, finally, a radiocarbon date of 33.0 ka to 35.5 ka was obtained. But obviously this radiocarbon date was too young to fit into their evolutionary timescale, so the researchers threw out this date, assuming that contamination must have occurred. In the end, they settled for a date of 236–335 ka. Evolution is assumed, and contradicting evidence is simply waved away.[97]" – Joel Tay

Take a look at the evolutionary "tree" on the Smithsonian's Human Origins web site. (Go to www.AJ83.com/tree). There are only branches. No fossils on the trunk. No fossils connecting the various branches. No transitions. None.

---

[95] Ibid page 173
[96] Ibid pages 125-126
[97] Joel Tay, "Do these skulls prove common ancestry between apes and humans?" (2018) - https://creation.com/ape-human-transitional-skull

Malaria: Are Random Mutations Beneficial?

We have already looked at the question of random mutations extensively and learned that random mutations result in devolution.

The best-known antimalarial mutation is the sickle-cell gene. It prevents malaria, but results in anemia, frequent infections, stroke, swelling of hands and feet, chronic pain, vision problems, and other medical issues. As the BBC said, in populations not exposed to malaria, the weakness resulting from sickle cell anemia eliminates people with that mutation. Michael Behe writes in Darwin Devolves:

> "Many other antimalaria mutations break genes or control regions. As malaria researchers have noted, in addition to their helpful effects the mutations have less benign consequences, most especially 'the great legacy of debilitating, and sometimes lethal, inherited diseases that have been selected under [malaria's] impact in the past.'"[98]

Yes, a random mutation can provide protection against malaria, but that is not evolution. While it provides a benefit, overall the mutation is debilitating. The person has gone downhill... devolved.

The comment about humans walking upright is pure bluster.

As the article admits, there is no evidence our upright stance evolved. And it is not as simple as a single mutation resulting in an upright stance, as the article implies. Upright walking is complex. It involves unique design features in the feet, legs, hips and other parts of the body. The BBC article is very misleading.

And the bottom line is, there is no evidence of an evolutionary source for our upright stance. The statement made in the BBC article is a form of the "Escape to Future" fallacy. Claiming the evidence is coming in the future, which is no evidence at all.

---

[98] Michael Behe, "Darwin Devolves", 2019, page 182

BBC's Proof of Human Evolution

Finally, say this aloud with no hint of doubt in your voice, "evolution is a fact of nature."

There, that is it. Evolution is a fact. In spite of the lack of evidence, you have declared it to be so. Making a declaration in a loud, clear voice, with no hint of doubt in your voice, makes it so.

No, evolution is not a fact. Declaring it to be a fact, without any solid, fact-based evidence, is meaningless.

CHAPTER 25
MIXED UP BONES

Most people picture paleontologists digging up complete, or nearly complete, skeletons that show the step-by-step progress of human evolution. There is an old Fat's Waller song that comes to mind:

> The toe bone's connected to the foot bone,
> The foot bone's connected to the ankle bone,
> The ankle bone's connected to the leg bone,
> Now shake dem skeleton bones!
> The leg bone's connected to the knee bone,
> The knee bone's connected to the thigh bone,
> The thigh bone's connected to the hip bone,
> Now shake dem skeleton bones!

That is how we picture fossils. They come out of the ground with all the pieces, and if not connected, the bones were at least close to each other. Paleontologists put them together, and then examine the result to see what can be learned. However, this is far... VERY FAR from what actually happens.

The bones used to assemble a skeleton may come from locations separated by several yards, or at times up to a mile or more.

Bones from a variety of animals and marine life, and including both ape and human bones, are frequently found all jumbled together. Scientists pick which bones go with which animal, and not all scientists pick the same bones. In some cases a skeleton is put together based more on a desire for the fame and fortune that comes

Mixed Up Bones

with finding a new transitional form, than it is based on what those bones actually represent.

Let's take a look at some of the famous "transitional" fossils in the human lineage.

Homo Habilis

> "This species, one of the earliest members of the genus Homo, has a slightly larger braincase and smaller face and teeth than in Australopithecus or older hominin species. But it still retains some ape-like features, including long arms and a moderately-prognathic face." – Smithsonian, National Museum of Natural History[99]

The above quote, describing Homo habilis, is the introductory paragraph of the Smithsonian's web page about Homo habilis. Because Habilis has a combination of ape and human features, it is thought to be in the lineage between Australopithecines (apes) and Homo erectus (human). However, here is the rest of the story quoted from the book "Contested Bones" by Christopher Rupe and Dr. John Sanford.

> "Ever since the naming of Habilis, there has been disquiet within the paleoanthropology community regarding whether or not Habilis was a sound species, and belonged in the genus Homo. The striking ape-like qualities of Habilis led many to conclude that Habilis bones are of the ape-type, not the human-type."[100]

> "Virtually all of the bones attributed to Habilis were found as isolated bones or bone fragments. None of the bones were found physically connected to other bones."[101]

> "The murky definition of what Habilis is has led to the uncritical inclusion of any unknown bones into the Habilis group. It is no wonder leading experts like Tattersall and Schwartz describe Habilis as an 'all-embracing watebasket species into which a whole heterogeneous variety of fossils could be conveniently swept.'"[102]

---

[99] https://humanorigins.si.edu/evidence/human-fossils/species/homo-habilis
[100] Christoher Rupe and Dr. John Sanford, "Contested Bones," (2019) page 160
[101] Ibid page 164
[102] Ibid pages 164-165

"Numerous lines of evidence suggest that Habilis is an invalid species, the product of active imaginations and fossil beds with both ape and human bones."[103]

"The invention of a 'new species' by combining bones from different species has occurred several times in the field of paleonanthropology. Paleo-experts acknowledge that it is not uncommon for hominin-bearing sites to contain a co-mixture of Homo and Australopithecus bones."[104]

Homo floresiensis - Homo erectus — Both Fully Human

A common problem with fossils attributed to the human lineage is that they are assembled from fossils beds containing both ape and human fossils. The result can be a fossil that is a mixture of ape and human bones and this, of course, looks like a transitional fossil. However, there is more. There are two other factors that lead to mischaracterization of fossils as ape-human transitions: pathologies and normal variation.

Homo floresiensis is so small that it is also known as "The Hobbit." Found in Indonesia, floresiensis stood just 3 feet 6 inches tall, had short femur bones (legs), and a cranial capacity of 420 cm^3. Here was a new human species that lived 18,000 years ago. Or, was it?

It is interesting that there are pygmies living on the same island, near the site where the Hobbit was found. Although the Hobbit fossil and the pygmies are not related, the conditions on the island lead to a pathologies resulting from island dwarfism, inbreeding, and reductive selection, collectively referred to as insular dwarfism Insular dwarfism is a well-known condition among mammals. It is described in the book "Contested Bones:"

"Mammals living on an island can become smaller over generations. This is typically seen in island-dwelling species with access to a limited food supply. Such dwarfed populations are reproductively isolated many generations, and must survive for long periods, undernourished and in very small populations."[105]

---

[103] Ibid page 169
[104] Ibid page 172
[105] Ibid page 88

Mixed Up Bones

The result is inbreeding, genetic drift, and deleterious mutations with selection favoring small size (as seen in the pygmies living there now). Homo floresiensis is fully within the known physical variation of humanity, with the pathologies expected from insula dwarfism. It is a fossil that appears to be very much like the pygmies currently living in that area.

Homo erectus

Homo erectus is claimed to be the oldest known early human. These fossils have modern human body proportions, body mass, and stature. They have a brain size within the range of modern human variation. They are associated with human abilities such as tool making and caring for elderly and weak individuals. Here is what the experts say:

> "The Homo erectus class first came into being by putting Java man (Pithecanthropus erectus), which consisted of the skull of a giant gorilla (or similar) and a human leg bone, together with Peking man (Sinanthropus pekinensis), composed entirely of ape skulls. To this was subsequently added a number of other skulls that were generally too human and too early a dating to class as apes, and therefore were put in this intermediate group." – Malcolm Bowden[106]

> "While Erectus is clearly human, it is not a normal human. Erectus was very much like Neanderthal--but displaying evidence of various pathologies. Many Erectus skulls are disturbing, showing diverse abnormalities and asymmetrics." – Christopher Rupe and Dr. John Sanford[107]

> "There is strong evidence that the bones commonly referred to as Homo erectus are fully human individuals who suffered from various pathologies associated with such things as inbreeding, mutation, teratogens (developmental abnormalities), etc... Indeed, most of the classic features attributed to Erectus--including those found in the skull and face--have been found in modern humans." – Christopher Rupe and Dr. John Sanford[108]

---

[106] Malcolm Bowden, "Homo Erectus – A Fabricated Class of 'Ape Men,'" https://tinyurl.com/yyj459s6
[107] Christoher Rupe and Dr. John Sanford, "Contested Bones," (2019) page 55
[108] Ibid page 77

Beginner's Guide To Tracking Dinosaurs

"Donald Johnson suggests that, were erectus alive today, it could mate with modern humans to produce fertile offspring. In other words, were it not for our separation by time, we might be considered interbreeding members of the same species. – Casey Luskin[109]"

What we actually have in the fossils that supposedly show human evolution are two, distinct types... humans and apes. The fossils claimed to be transitional are fully human with either normal variation or pathologies, or even fully human with a few ape bones mixed in. I will address the ape-like fossils, such as Lucy, beginning in chapter 29.

An excellent book that looks at this subject in-depth is "Contested Bones" by Christoher Rupe and Dr. John Sanford

A final quote from Casey Luskin to finish this chapter:

"Despite the claims of evolutionary paleoanthropologists and unceasing media hype, the fragmented hominin fossil record does not document the evolution of humans from ape-like precursors. While the hominin fossil record is marked by incomplete and fragmented fossils, known hominins fall into two separate groups: ape-like and human-like, with a distinct gap between them. The genus *Homo* appears in an abrupt, non-Darwinian fashion, without evidence of an evolutionary transition from ape-like hominins. Other members of *Homo* appear very similar to modern humans."[110]

---

[109] Casey Luskin, "Theistic Evolution", "Missing Transition: Human Origins and the Fossil Record," Crossway, (2017) page 469. Quoting: Donald C. Johnson and Maitland Edey, "Lucy, The Beginnings of Humankind," Simon & Schuster, (1981), page 144

[110] Casey Luskin, "Theistic Evolution", "Missing Transition: Human Origins and the Fossil Record," Crossway, (2017) page 472

Mixed Up Bones

CHAPTER 26
TRUST JESUS, NOT DARWIN

I have been showing that the evidence supports what the Bible records about a global flood, and the evidence does not support evolution as actually having happened. This leads to the question, what does the evidence say about the Bible and Jesus?

Should you trust Jesus or Darwin?

To the right is a sign from our museum that presents a dichotomy. Jesus or Darwin? That IS the question. At the bottom it states that Darwin was proven wrong over 50 years ago, at the end of the 1960's. There is a URL in the small print (www.SciencePastor.com/darwin) at the bottom of the sign, It takes you to one of our web pages that supports this claim. To give you a quick summary, by the end of the 1960's we had learned enough about biology, the cell, and genetics such that many leading scientists

concluded that life is much too complex to have evolved through random mutations.

However, that is not news to us. We (all humans) have all known the truth long before the 1960's. From the beginning, God has made it plainly evident to us:

> "For the wrath of God is revealed from heaven against all ungodliness and unrighteousness of men who suppress the truth in unrighteousness, because that which is known about God is evident within them; for God made it evident to them. For since the creation of the world His invisible attributes, His eternal power and divine nature, have been clearly seen, being understood through what has been made, so that they are without excuse. For even though they knew God, they did not honor Him as God or give thanks, but they became futile in their speculations, and their foolish heart was darkened. Professing to be wise, they became fools." - Romans 1:18-22

God has made Himself known to us through His creation. However, we suppress that knowledge. In our pride, we want to be the ones who are in charge, not God.

However, that anything at all exists is powerful evidence that God exists. A common analogy is that of a painting. You are visiting a museum and see a painting hanging on the wall. Where did that painting come from? Someone had to paint it. If there is a painting, we know there is a painter. Where did the museum building come from? There was a builder. We intuitively know that if there is a painting, there has to be a painter. If there is a building, there has to be a builder. Since there is a creation, there has to be a creator. Something does not come from nothing. (The law of causality.)

Does Science Disprove The Bible!

I have been debunking evolution and the idea that the present is the key to the past. We have seen that evolution is not be supported by the evidence. What about the Bible? Christianity is based on the Bible. Is the Bible accurate in all it teaches? Has science shown the Bible has numerous errors? What does the evidence say?

Unlike other religions, Christianity is based in factual history. The Bible claims to be a record of real people and real events. The

Beginner's Guide To Tracking Dinosaurs

Bible tells us about the Creator who made everything, and that He did it by speaking everything into existence. The Bible is true in all that it asserts to be true. Is this statement correct?

Let's Ask a Humanist

To put it to a test, and find out if the Bible is true in all that it asserts to be true, I went to the American Humanist web site. Who better to turn to when looking for errors or contradictions in the Bible? They have a long web page that attempts to prove the Bible is full of historical and scientific errors, as well as contradictions and outright immoral actions on the part of God. I read it all. As best as I could count, there are 180 accusations against the Bible. Every one was false, a misrepresentation of scripture, or a misuse of history.

I actually wrote down the answers to each one of their accusations. I would put those answers in this chapter, except they took about 400 pages to write out. You can read them in a two-volume book called *"Answers to 180 Humanist Accusations Against the Bible."* It is available on Amazon. It is also available for downloading (PDF) free on my web site. Here is the link:

www.sciencepastor.com/books/atheist.php

The bottom line is that, yes, the Bible IS ACCURATE in all that it teaches. And, NO, science does not prove there are errors in the Bible. For 2000 years, the Bible has withstood attacks and attempts to destroy it. It has never been proven to be in error. For example, let's take a quick look at the issue of scientific errors. I have divided the possible errors into three categories.

(1) The presumption that that miracles are impossible, and thus are unscientific.

This is not a scientific objection, but a metaphysical one. Miracles are miracles because they violate the physical "laws." God, who created everything, including the physical laws, can certainly do that. This is not an objection to miracles in the Bible, it is an objection to God. Yet, the miracles in the Bible provide powerful proofs God does exist, is real, and that Jesus is God (see the Gospel of John).

Trust Jesus Not Darwin

How do we know Jesus' miracles were real?

The miracles were done in public with many eyewitnesses. They are recorded in writing in an environment in which those in power (the Jewish leadership) wanted to discredit and even kill off all Christians. What better way to discredit Christianity than to reveal Christians as fakes and liars? If Jesus' miracles did not happen, the people in the crowds who followed him would have proclaimed, "He didn't do those things!" However, they couldn't. And the Jewish leaders could not deny the miracles. They had even been present and seen some of them themselves! There were too many eyewitnesses who saw the miracles. The written record in the Gospels was circulated during the lifetimes of the eyewitnesses. The miracles could not be denied. The miracles were real. They did happen. And they were things only God can do.

(2) Statements in the Bible about the physical world contradict what science says.

These are accusations that need to be addressed individually. Each typically has an answer based in its Biblical context. Some are the result of misreading what scripture says, and others are the result of misrepresenting scripture or Christianity.

The following is an example of what humanists claimed is scientific error in the Bible:

The Bible supports a flat earth supported on pillars.

The humanists support this claim by showing the Bible talks about the four corners of the earth, for example Isaiah 11:12. That means the Bible is saying the earth is flat and has four corners. The humanists also claim the Bible states the earth is held in place by pillars (1 Samuel 2:8).

You can probably answer these. The "four corners of the earth" is a common expression used to say "everywhere." It is an expression we still use today and it has nothing to do with claiming the earth is flat.

In 1ˢᵗ Samuel 2:8 the context is that of God talking about people, not the earth. Scripture is saying that God stabilizes societies (not the physical planet earth) through the "pillars" of His common grace and His laws. This is a common way we use the word "pillar" today. For example, a pillar of industry is a person who is highly influential and respected in business.

Every example the humanists mention was easily refuted, just as this one was.

(3) There are contradictory statements in the Bible about the physical world.

For example, the humanists claim that God does not know the difference between birds and bats. They reference Leviticus 11:13-19 for this one.

God knows the difference between birds and bats. He created them. What the humanists miss is that God does not use human created systems for categorizing life. God is not required to follow our rules.

This is an important fact to remember. Humanity has established a system we use to categorize all life. It is a human created categorization system. However, God is not required to create life forms according to our system of categorizing life. On page 139 I talked about the platypus. It has characteristics of mammals, reptiles and birds. It is an animal that does not fit into any one category. So we put it a category all; by itself. Another human created category.

In Genesis one we see that God does have categories, but they are not the same as human created categories.

Plants - Genesis 1:11
Living creatures in the water – Genesis 1:20-21
Winged creatures that fly above earth – Genesis 1:20-21
Domesticated land animals (livestock) – Genesis 1:24
Animals of the earth – Genesis 1:24
Land animals that crawl – Genesis 1:24
Humanity – Genesis 1:26-27

The humanists complain that Leviticus 11 calls a bat a bird. However, that is what we read in English using our assumption that bats and birds are in different categories. God's category is "winged creatures that fly." Both bats and birds are in that category. The Bible is not in error.

The humanist's are wrong. There are no scientific errors in the Bible. The Bible can be trusted. It is true in all that it asserts to be true. Put your trust in Jesus, not Darwin.

CHAPTER 27
WHO MADE GOD?

Who made God? This question is frequently raised when it is pointed out to believers in evolution that, with the Big Bang, they are believing nothing created everything. So they say, "If the Big Bang has to come from something, so does your God." It is not difficult to get the answer. The answer is all over the web. This question seems to be asked more as an attempt to stump Christians… a gotcha question. "Christian. You can't answer this question, eh? Well then! Don't claim the Big Bang needs a creator, if you can't tell me who made God."

The Law of Causality: Every Event Has a Cause.

Because we live within the realm of time, every event has a beginning. Everything that has a beginning has to have a cause. And that, of course, includes the universe. The universe exists within time. We see that in Einstein's famous equation that describes the relationship of everything in the universe, $E=MC^2$. "C" is the speed of light, 186,000 miles/second. Speed, distance divided by time, cannot exist outside of space and time. There have been more sophisticated proofs than this, but even this simple equation reveals that for mass, energy and space (distance) to exist, time must exist. And since the universe had a beginning, so did time.

Who Made God?

The law of causality applies to events within time, and since time began when the universe began, it must have a cause and that cause must be outside of the universe and thus outside of time.

The Cause of the Universe

What characteristics would the cause of the universe (and time) have to have?

(1) **Exist outside of time.** That means the cause is eternal.

(2) **All powerful.** The universe has a billion galaxies, each with a billion stars, and there is more to the universe than the galaxies. The cause of the universe has to be not simply powerful, but all powerful.

(3) **Non-material (spirit).** Since the cause creates all material things, the cause cannot be material.

(4) **Incredibly intelligent.** Design can be seen throughout the universe. The cause would have to conceive of this design, conceive of what we call the natural laws, figure out how it will all interact and work together, plan it all and then cause it all to happen. That takes intelligence beyond our imagination.

It is impossible for finite beings like us to know the mind of such an incredible creator-cause of our universe. However, it seems logical that the creator-cause, having intentionally created intelligent living beings (us), would provide a means for us to learn about and know the creator-cause's creation.

He has....

God has created a universe designed in such a way such that we can study it, observe it, and learn what it is and how it works, and from that learn about God. There are many examples. One of my favorites is the relationship of the earth, moon and sun. The moon is exactly the right size, and the right distance away from the earth to

Beginner's Guide To Tracking Dinosaurs

block the disk of the sun during an eclipse. This also requires the sun to be the right size and the earth-moon system to be just the right distance from the sun. Because the moon perfectly blocks the disk of the sun during an eclipse, we are able to observe the sun and learn things about the sun that we otherwise (if the distances and sizes were just a little bit different) not be able to learn.

Evolution postulates that everything came about through random chance. Life evolved as the result of random mutations selected by natural selection. The universe is the result of an explosion out of which stars and planetary bodies condensed, with no specific design or purpose. And out of all this randomness life developed, in spite of the overwhelming probability against that happening, and it developed on the rarest of rare planets. A planet that has a single moon that is perfect for allowing life on that planet to study their sun. These are impossibilities piled on impossibilities.

No. It did not randomly happen. The designer's fingerprints are all over the universe. Not only are the earth-moon-and sun designed in a way such that we can study and learn about God's creation. Our position in the galaxy and our galaxy's location in the universe makes it possible for us to study the universe. God has given us a universe we can study, and from this we learn about His invisible attributes, His eternal power and divine nature.[111]

Without a creator-cause we end up having to pick from three options:

(A) Turtles all the way down. This was the mythological idea that the earth was supported on the back of a turtle (or elephant). What supported that turtle? It stood on the back of another turtle. And what supported that one? It stood on the

---

[111] To learn about the fine tuning of the universe, see: https://creation.com/the-universe-is-finely-tuned-for-life

back of still another turtle. It is turtles all the way down. This is what is called an infinite regress, and is obviously not realistic.

(B) Everything came from nothing. It has been interesting to watch evolution evangelists try to define nothing as something, but nothing MEANS nothing. It is obvious that something does not come from nothing. This option is also not realistic.

(C) Everything came from something, but we do not know what that something is. In this assertion we have total blind faith. It is a faith that there is something out there that is outside of time, and both unimaginably powerful and intelligent, but that something is not the God of the Bible and it does not want its creation to know it exists. This option requires an incredible amount of faith in the unknown.

If you do not believe in God, which of these three options do you choose? "A" and ""B" are absurd. That leaves "C." Believing in a god-like entity for which there is no evidence except… that the universe was obviously created by something. And then you are going to tell me you don't believe in the God of the Bible because you believe in some other god-like cause for which there is no evidence? Huh? Let's examine that…

We know there is a creator-cause. There has to be. What means would He use to let us know He exists and what He is like?

The Creator Cause Revealed

There are two ways we learn about things. We directly observe the physical world around us and learn from experience, and we read and learn from what others before us have learned. The creator cause uses both of these methods, revealing to us that He is the great I AM.

Revealed Through His Creation

"For the wrath of God is revealed from heaven against all ungodliness and unrighteousness of men who suppress the truth in unrighteousness, because that which is known about God is evident within

*them; for God made it evident to them. For since the creation of the world **His invisible attributes, His eternal power and divine nature, have been clearly seen, being understood through what has been made, so that they are without excuse.** For even though they knew God, they did not honor Him as God or give thanks, but they became futile in their speculations, and their foolish heart was darkened. Professing to be wise, they became fools."* - Romans 1:18-22

Revealed Through His Word

The creator cause has also revealed Himself through a written record. Through His word (the Bible) He is revealed as the one we simply call God. That is not His name. Since He is the one and only God, that is all we need to say. God. The creator of the universe, everything physical and even time itself. God has no beginning, because God exists outside of time. Therefore, God has no cause. Everything that exists came from God, the eternal, all-powerful, non-material, incredibility intelligent uncreated I AM.

Through His creation we learn that God exists and has the characteristics the creator of everything must have. Through His word we learn who He is; what He has done; and who we are (His image bearers, making us incredibly unique); the problem we have (sin); and what HE has done to solve that problem (the cross).

The Uncreated Creator

(1) Exists outside of time (eternal).
God was already there at the beginning. *"In the beginning was the Word [Jesus], and the Word was with God, and the Word was God"* - John 1:1

(2) All powerful.
"For the Lord your God is the God of gods and the Lord of lords, the great, the mighty, and the awesome God who does not show partiality nor take a bribe." - Deuteronomy 10:17

(3) Non-material (spirit).
" God is spirit, and those who worship Him must worship in spirit and truth." - John 4:24

(4) Incredibly intelligent (omniscient).

Who Made God?

"For God is greater than our heart and knows all things." - 1 John 3:20
The great I AM. The uncreated creator of the universe and all that is in it... including you.

(5) He is the source of truth.
"Jesus said to him, 'I am the way, and the truth, and the life. No one comes to the Father except through me.'" – John 14:6

CHAPTER 28
WHO IS LUCY?

Lucy has been promoted as a human ancestor to a greater degree than any other fossil. Who is Lucy? Is she a human ancestor? Let's start by seeing what a popular high school biology textbook has to say about Lucy:

> "One early group of hominines, of the genus *Australopithecus,* lived about 4 million to about 1.5 million years ago. These hominines were bipedal apes, but their skeletons suggest that they probably spent at least some time in trees. ...
>
> "The best-known of these species is *Australopithecus afarensis,* which lived roughly 4 million to 2.5 million years ago. The humanlike footprints in figure 26-17[112], about 3.6 million years old, were probably made by members of this species. *A. afarensis* fossils indicate the species had small brains, so the footprints show that hominines walked bipedally long before large brains evolved."[113]

Australopithicus afarensis, that is Lucy, is the most famous fossil ever found. We have a cast of the Lucy fossil in our museum. We also have a cast of a small section of the footprints, referred to as fig. 26-27 in the above quote, known as the Laetoli footprints. We will be looking at those in chapter 31.

---

[112] These are the Laetoli footprints that I'll discuss in chapter 31
[113] Miller & LeVine, "Biology," (2010), page 768, emphasis as in the original

Who Is Lucy?

We need to ask a question we should never have to ask about a High School textbook: How much of this is fact and how much is fiction?

Is Lucy A Human Ancestor?

Lucy is no longer thought to be a human ancestor. Humans and Australopithecus afarenis are thought to have a common ancestor, but humans are not thought to have descended from A. afarensis. Human evolutionary history is now thought of like a bush, with many branches representing human related species. However, there are no fossils showing direct evolutionary steps from apes to humans.[114]

In their book "Bones of Contention" (page 115), Christopher Rupe and Dr. John Sanford describe some of the history of Lucy and how she became famous.

> "According to his colleagues, Johanson" [the paleontologist who found the Lucy fossils] "loved the media spotlight and was a "publicity hound." He was able to win over the media and influence a sizeable portion of the field as he promoted his own person interpretation of the Hadar-Laetoli findings." [this refers to the Laetoli footprints he thought were made by Lucy's relatives] ... "As you will see, many leading paleo-experts have rejected Johanson's claims about Afarensis as a sound species and the ancestor to us all."

Could it be that the famous fossil is more about marketing and promotional skills than it is about science?

The Evidence:
Humans and A. Afarensis (Lucy) Coexisted

If you base your conclusions on what is seen on TV and taught in public schools, it appears as though paleontologists dig in the dirt in East Africa, and sometimes find an ancient human relative such as Lucy. However, that is not what happens. Fossil bones are more often found in a jumble of bones from various animals, including australopith bones and homo (human) bones. Some of the bones used to put

---

[114] See my 30 second video: www.AJ83.com/tree

together a fossil skeleton may be found hundreds of feet or even a mile apart. The paleontologist looks at all the bones and figures out which bones go with which animal. Based on evolutionary assumptions that humans did not exist 3 to 4 million years ago, it is assumed that any human looking bones must actually be australopith bones... because obviously humans had not yet evolved into existence. The resulting australopith skeleton, put together from scattered bones, is actually part ape bones and part human bones... a supposed evolutionary transition that "proves" human evolution happened.

In What Condition Was Lucy Found?

Christopher Rupe and Dr. John Sanford write:

> "The disconnect bones attributed to Lucy were scattered and loose, fragmentary bones that were eroding out of the hillside. ... Additional recovered bones that were presumed to belong to the Lucy skeleton were found only after sifting mass amounts" [20 tons] "of sediment covering an area of roughly 50 square meters."[115] [~540 sq ft]

Human & Other Australopith Bones Found Together

> "At the core of this ongoing debate is the widely-recognized observation that some of the postcranial bones in the Afarensis hypodigm" [type] "look distinctly like apes, whereas other postcranial bones look distinctly like modern humans."[116]

> "The Leaky team and the Johanson team were consistently finding australopith bones in the same strata as human bones, along with human tools, human shelters, and human footprints. These findings were obvious to all, but were disturbing because the pattern did not reveal an ape-to-man progression. ... Johanson resolved this dilemma by asserting that all bones older than 3 million years must always be designated australopith, even when they are indistinguishable from human bones, and even if they were corroborated by human footprints."[117]

---

[115] Christopher Rupe and Dr. John Sanford, "Bones of Contention," (2019) page 125
[116] Ibid page 146
[117] Ibid page 152

Who Is Lucy?

It appears the actual observable evidence does not carry any weight when it contradicts evolutionary beliefs. What is Lucy? She is an ape, possibly a bonobo or similar type of ape.

> "Lucy's discoverer, Donald Johanson, admitted that her bones were found scattered across a hillside. His written account quotes Lucy-researcher Tim White further explaining how the bones were not found together: 'Since the fossil wasn't found in situ, it could have come from anywhere above. There's no matrix on any of the bones we've found either. All you can do is make probability statements [that Lucy was a single individual.]"[118]

> "Paleoanthropologists Leslie Aiello states that when it comes to locomotion, 'australopithecines [Lucy] are like apes, and the Homo group are like humans. Something major occurred when Homo evolved, and it wasn't just in the brain.' That 'something major' was the abrupt appearance of the human-like body plan—without direct evolutionary precursors in the fossil record."[119] – Casey Luskin

What Luskin is saying in the above is that, there is no evidence of human evolution from apes. Humans seem to have just appeared in the fossil record in our full modern form. The most likely reason for this is that humans have always been humans.

Why do humans "suddenly appear?" It might be because when human fossils are found in sediment dating to be older than about three millions years, they are ignored (file drawered), discarded, or reclassified as anything but human.

---

[118] Casey Luskin, "Theistic Evolution", "Missing Transition: Human Origins and the Fossil Record," Crossway, (2017) page 451
[119] Ibid page 455

CHAPTER 29
IS LUCY SAVED?

If Lucy is a human ancestor, could she sin? Was her sin covered by the blood of Jesus? If humans evolved from apes, at what point did we become responsible for our sin?

Could Lucy sin? No, she was an ape. Animals cannot sin.

Who is capable of sin? Only humans. Only humans rebel against God. Only humans are created in the image of God and are responsible for obeying God. As God's image bearers we are unique and special. However, along with that we have the responsibility to show God's character by obeying God (the Ten Commandments for example[120]). Jesus, in His incarnation, fully and completely obeyed God.

"Jesus said to them, "My food is to do the will of Him who sent Me and to accomplish His work." - John 4:34

We are to be like Jesus.

If evolution is true (it is not), and we are related to Lucy (we are not) who is an animal, at what point in the progress of evolution did mankind take on the image of God? If evolution is true, we cannot

---
[120] God never gives commandments for animals.

Is Lucy Saved?

go to scripture for the answer. Scripture describes God as creating everything in six days, including creating the first man and woman on the sixth day, the same day land animals were created. It says nothing about a point in time at which an ape (an animal) became a human. According to scripture, humans were human from the beginning.

Wouldn't God Tell Us?

Why has God given us the Bible? In scripture God tells us about ourselves, who we are, and the situation we are in (fallen sinners). And He tells us about Himself and what He has done about the situation we are in (the cross). God is not playing guessing games. He straight out tells us what the situation is. So, if we have evolved from some other living thing, would that not be a significant part of the story?

Moreover, if humanity did not came into existence until about 3 million years ago, that means sin could not have come into the world until about 3 million years ago. Since it was sin that brought death, this means death did not come into the world until about 3 million years ago.

> *"Just as through one man sin entered into the world, and death through sin, and so death spread to all men, because all sinned"* - Romans 5:12

There was no death in the world until a man (Adam) sinned. Yet evolution happens through random mutations and natural selection. Natural selection uses death to select those best fit to survive. That seems to bring us into a catch-22. Evolution requires death in order to select "improvements." However, humanity supposedly requires evolution to be functioning so that humans can evolve into existence. The pieces of this puzzle are not fitting together. Do you see the problem? You have to choose either Darwin or Jesus. And Darwin isn't looking too good.

Either evolution is right or the Bible is right. Trying to fit evolution and billions of years into the Bible does not work. God did not use evolution as a creative tool. There are only two options. Molecules to man evolution, or what the Bible says in a plain reading of scripture. Considering that neither the Bible nor the evidence supports evolution. What are we left with?

> *In the beginning GOD created the heavens and the earth...*
>
> *Then the LORD God formed the man of dust from the ground, and breathed into his nostrils the breath of life; and the man became a living person.*
>
> *The LORD God commanded the man, saying, "From any tree of the garden you may freely eat; but from the tree of the knowledge of good and evil you shall not eat, for on the day that you eat from it you will certainly die."*
>
> *When the woman saw that the tree was good for food, and that it was a delight to the eyes, and that the tree was desirable to make one wise, she took some of its fruit and ate; and she also gave some to her husband with her, and he ate.*
>
> *Just as through one man sin entered into the world, and death through sin, and so death spread to all men, because all sinned.*
>
> *For as through the one man's disobedience the many were made sinners, so also through the obedience of the One the many will be made righteous.*
>
> *Now if we have died with Christ, we believe that we shall also live with Him, knowing that Christ, having been raised from the dead, is never to die again; death no longer is master over Him. For the death that He died, He died to sin once for all time; but the life that He lives, He lives to God. So you too, consider yourselves to be dead to sin, but alive to God in Christ Jesus.*

Is Lucy Saved?

CHAPTER 30
THE LAETOLI FOOTPRINTS

Location: Olduvai Gorge in Tanzania.

The rock: dated to be 3.6 million years old.

Evolution states: Humans (Homo habillis) evolved into existence about 2.5 million years ago.

Fact: There are human fossil footprints in this 3.6 million year old rock. There is no disagreement, these are clearly human footprints.

Analysis of the Evidence: These are human footprints, so a human must have walked here.

Evolutionary Conclusion: The Laetoli footprints were made by an ape-like Australopith, not by a human. (Huh?)

    What is Going On? There is a firm rule that may not be violated: The physical evidence cannot contradict evolutionary theory. If there is a conflict between the observable evidence and evolutionary theory, reinterpret the evidence to create a new conclusion that does not conflict with evolutionary theory.

    Have you ever wondered why scientists have "never found" evidence of humans living tens of millions years ago? By definition that is an impossibility, without regard to what the evidence shows.

The Laetoli Footprints

"The paradigm [evolution] will consistently take precedence over the data."[121] In no instance... under no circumstances will the evidence be allowed to contradict evolutionary theory. Evolution rules, the physical evidence must be adapted to the theory.

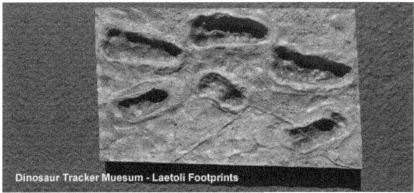

Figure 45 – Reproduction of the Laetoli (human) footprints in our museum.

Laetoli Human Footprints

Human footprints are unique. Our big toes point straight ahead, in line with the foot. We do not have claws. Our foot has a stiff structure designed for the strong push-off needed for bipedal movement. We have an arched foot that leaves strong impressions of the heel and balls of our feet. Human footprints are unlike those of any other living creature.

The Laetoli footprints were discovered by Mary Leakey's team in the late 1980's. They were analyzed by University of Chicago professor Russell Tuttle. In 1990 he concluded that the *"footprint trails at Laetoli site G resemble those of habitually unshod modern humans."* While this, because of their age, strongly conflicts with evolutionary theory, it perfectly fits with a Biblical flood. Humans have lived with all of the other land animals, including australopiths (apes) and dinosaurs, since day six of creation.

---

[121] Christopher Rupe and Dr. John Sanford, "Bones of Contention," (2019) page 287

Beginner's Guide To Tracking Dinosaurs

Are These the Oldest Human Footprints?

The Laetoli footprints are not the oldest human footprints. Footprints in Crete discovered in 2002 and announced in a paper published in the Proceedings of the Geologist Association in 2017, were named the Trachilos footprints. These human footprints are dated at 5.7 million years old. Why did it take 15 years to get a paper published? In a CBC news interview[122] the discovers explained,

> "We got ferociously aggressive responses saying this couldn't possibly be true and these can't be footprints at all... There would be at least one, and sometimes several reviewers who were in the first instance savagely hostile. ... Basically, it wasn't a true peer review process at all. They were just trying to shut us down."

Have you ever wondered why paleontologists have "never found" evidence of humans living more than 3 or 4 million years ago? By evolutionary standards that is impossible, and if found, it certainly cannot be published.

My guess is that even now, years later, you have not heard that human footprints, predating supposed human evolution by 3 million years (based on evolutionary dating) have been found.

Observable Evidence vs. Blind Faith

We can look at the footprint evidence. There are human footprints in Laetoli, Tanzania that are over 3 million years old. There are human footprints in Crete, that are nearly 6 million years old... ages based on evolutionary thinking and testing, that bust evolutionary theory. Do you believe the evidence?

On the other hand, you can have a blind faith in evolution and ignore or trivialize the evidence. It is your choice. You get to decide whether reality is based on truth or an illusion. Or do you get to decide? Can what you believe change reality?

We have seen that dinosaur footprints require very special conditions in order for them to be fossilized. Yet, there are billions of dinosaur footprints around the world (and raindrop impressions). All

---

[122] https://newsinteractives.cbc.ca/longform/human-footprints-greece

The Laetoli Footprints

as a result of conditions that only a global flood could produce. Flat mud bedding planes that go on for miles with no vegetation. The evidence is overwhelming. There are continent spanning sediment layers, folded rock layers, and more. The evidence is truly overwhelming. (www.SciencePastor.com/flood) The fossil and sediment record cries out, "Evolution never happened! There was a global flood!"

CHAPTER 31
SUPPRESS ALL OPPOSITION

Location: Nash Dinosaur Track Quarry, Massachusetts

Research Subject: Carbon Dating Dinosaur Footprints)

The rock: evolution-based dated to be about 180 million years old.

    Carbon dating can only be used to date organic materials that contain carbon. Dinosaur tracks in shale cannot be carbon dated... except for... some of the tracks from the Nash Quarry... and we have them in our museum. The shale in the Nash Quarry has an unusually high level of embedded vegetation. Most of it is fossilized meaning they are fossil impressions of the vegetation. These are stone and cannot be carbon dated.
    However, at the Nash Quarry, in rare instances, some of the small pieces of wood became coalified. The wood became coal instead of fossilizing. Coal is carbon and can be carbon dated. That means the dinosaur tracks in the same rock can be carbon dated.
    In 2013 I collected shale with coalified wood from the Nash Quarry. The coalified wood can be seen as small dark gray and black areas in the stone shown in figure 46. You can also see fossilized wood impressions. I used dental tools to remove a sufficient amount of coalified wood for carbon dating. We have the money to pay for carbon dating. However, I have yet to find a carbon dating lab that will do the work. Most will not accept samples from someone who is

Suppress All Opposition

not associated with a university or recognized research facility. Those that would do the dating for us have a clause in their contract that excludes dating of samples that have anything to do with dinosaurs. We would become liable for all damages and costs associated with their having dated the samples. That means if evolutionists raise a ruckus, and they will, we have to pay for the attorneys as well as any awards or settlements. We do not have that kind of money.

Figure 46 – Coalified wood found in the same rock as dinosaur tracks.

Why Don't they want to do the Carbon Dating?

Radioactive carbon 14 only lasts 100,000 years. If any carbon 14 is found, that means the dinosaur footprint has to be considerably less than 100,000 years old. Many dinosaur bones have been tested and carbon 14 has been found in every one. That is strong evidence that either carbon 14 dating is not reliable, or dinosaurs lived recently. Neither result is acceptable to evolutionists. So what do they do? Take the data at face value and figure out the reason for the young age? No. Sweep the data under the carpet (ignore it) and take steps to ensure no further tests are done? YES!

It is unfortunate that there are some labs willing to do the dating, but they are being bullied by evolutionists who create a fear of potential lawsuits and the loss of business due to ad-hominin attacks.

In the previous chapter about the Laetoli footprints we learned that, if your results do not agree with evolutionary thinking, it is very difficult to get published. Now we see that, if the results are likely to disagree with evolutionary thinking, it is very difficult to get testing

Beginner's Guide To Tracking Dinosaurs

done[123]. A landmark documentary film, *"Expelled: No Intelligence Allowed"* documents some of the ways people and information are suppressed. It is available on YouTube. Here is the link:

https://youtu.be/V5EPymcWp-g

Many dinosaur bones have been tested and most carbon date to be between 25,000 and 35,000 years old. That does not mean this is the actual age, but it does demonstrate they are not millions of years old. (Carbon dating has proven to be unreliable for older dates. See www.SciencePastor.com/evidence2)

Here are some examples of dinosaur bones that have been carbon dated:

- Hadrosaur - Hell Creek Formation: 28,790 years
- Edmontodsaurus - Lance Formation: 25,550 years
- Hadrosaur - Hell Creek Formation: 20,850 years
- Ceratopsian - Horseshoe Canyon Formation: 26,300 years
- Edmontosaurus - Lance Formation: 32,420 years
- Hadrosaur - Horseshoe Canyon Formation: 32,770 years

The observable evidence is clear. Dinosaurs lived recently, not millions of years ago. They left their footprints in soft sediment thousands of years ago, during Noah's flood, not millions of years ago.

---

[123] Why not have the testing done by a laboratory operated by Christians? There are two reasons. The equipment and staff needed for a radiometric dating lab is expensive, making it difficult for Biblical scientists, who have little funding, to establish such a lab. And secondarily, the secular world would not accept the results. They will claim the lab is biased and as a result produces false results. To date dinosaur bone testing has all been done by secular labs, using their procedures and requirements, and all show dinosaur bones to be recent, not millions of years old.

Suppress All Opposition

CHAPTER 32
PETRIFIED TREES

Figure 47 – Stumps with no roots in a petrified "forest."

Location: Theodore Roosevelt National Park, North Dakota.

The above photo shows a large petrified tree stump, with two others in the background. Notice the three stumps are on top of the same layer of sediment. A fourth stump looks as though it fell from the same level as the sediment eroded away. Notice something else... there are no roots. All of these stumps were ripped off their roots. Anyone who has ever removed a stump knows this is nearly impossible to do. What happened?

Another question: This is called a petrified forest, because to some people it looks like a forest grew here. We see the stumps and

Petrified Trees

that petrified logs are scattered around the area. However, that does not mean there was a forest. And besides, how could trees with no roots grow, or even stand upright? This was not a forest. Something else happened here. What was it?

May 1981 Mt. St. Helens Erupted... And Gave Us Answers

The eruption of Mt. St. Helens caused massive mud flows that ripped trees off their roots. The rootless trees were carried into Spirit Lake where they floated. As they became water-logged, the heavier stump end of the log sank, tilting some logs into an upright position. The logs sank to the bottom of the lake, burying the stump end in the mud, and leaving the tree standing upright. A "forest" of trees on the bottom of Sprit Lake!

However, Mt. St. Helens showed us something else. Not all trees ended up in Spirit Lake. Some were carried by the mud flows to other locations, and remained embedded in the mud flow:

> "This volcanic debris included enormous quantities of trees which had been devastated and stripped of their branches and leaves.
>
> "Reporting the event, Fritz[5] stated that many of the trees from Mount St. Helens were transported many kilometers down Toutle Canyon by ash and mudflows and deposited upright and at various other angles. Fritz commented (and recorded by photography) that although all the blasted stumps were devoid of branches, many still had large root systems. Some even retained fine rootlets. This was true particularly for the shorter stumps, which were deposited upright in an apparent growth position. The longer logs were often deposited horizontally while some were in diagonal position.[124]"

Mud flows during a global flood would have been orders of magnitude greater than the Mt. St. Helens mud flows. They would have uprooted, carried and quickly buried trees. There are some lessons here:

(1) Trees in a petrified "forest" without roots were obviously transported from another location.

---

[124] Fritz, W.J., Stumps transported and deposited upright by Mount St. Helens mud flows, *Geology* 8:586–588, 1980, quoted by: Dr. Andrew Snelling and John Mackay, "Coal, Volcanism and Noah's Flood," Ex Nihilo Journal, April 1984

Beginner's Guide To Tracking Dinosaurs

(2) Some trees in petrified" forests may still have roots. We cannot assume natural events always produce the exact same results. The character of the natural event, the location, the environment, and the circumstance are unique.

(3) As with identifying dinosaur tracks, we need to look at all the evidence, and determine the story a preponderance of the evidence supports. Evidence that a tree was transported before being petrified includes no roots, missing branches and leaf structures, and the ends of the trunks being fractured (broken off). Not all of these will be present in every circumstance.

An example of additional evidence is seen in petrified "forests" where some standing petrified trees are 30 feet tall. How could a tree that tall become petrified standing upright? Petrification requires burial in sediment, in this case over 30 feet of sediment. A tree will not stand unchanged while 30 feet of sediment accumulates over a long period of time. On the other hand, a global flood could easily and quickly bury a tree in 30 feet or more of sediment.

We must not stop thinking when we have an answer we like. We must be sure we have considered all the evidence, and that we correctly understand that evidence. For example, in other locations, with different types of trees and sediment, we see something different.

Polystrate Trees

Depending on the situation and type of tree, when hit with flood waters or mud flows trees will break in different ways (if they break). The stumps in figure 47 broke off at the roots. Other trees may break off higher up on the trunk and leave part of the trunk, the stump and roots behind.

Even in a global flood most trees will not be buried in sediment and be petrified. The vast coal beds of America were originally vegetation. The massive sediment flows early on in the global flood probably stripped the vegetation off the land, and quickly and deeply buried it. This created tremendous pressure and heat, converting the

Petrified Trees

vegetation to coal. As the flood water drained off the land the rushing water eroded away (sheet erosion) thousands of feet of sediment making the coal accessible to us today.

However, in a few instances tree trunks were buried upright in sediment. That sediment became hard rock. We see them today... fossil trees that vertically go through many layers of rock hard sediment that supposedly took thousands of years to be deposited. Do you see what is wrong with this picture? A tree will not last thousands of years while sediment builds up around it. For polystrate trees to exist, and they do in multiple locations, the tree must be buried quickly and deeply, as would happen in a global flood.

Similar to petrified stumps, polystrate trees at times have no roots nor branches[125]. If these trees died standing in place, they would have roots and branches. However, if the trees were broken off by massive flood waters, carried away, sank heavy end down, and then were buried... exactly what would happen in a global flood... then polystrate trees with no roots and branches make sense.

Figure 48 - Reproduction of a polystrate tree at the Creation Evidence Museum of Texas

What Do Dead Clams Tell Us?

Location: Oregon Coast Range

The photo on the next page shows open mussel shells and dead clams that are closed. The mussel shells were collected recently, the closed clams are fossils.

---

[125] Some polystrate trees do have a root or roots still attached. To see a photo go to: www.dinosaurtracker.com/polystrate

Beginner's Guide To Tracking Dinosaurs

A clam's muscles keep the clam shell closed. When a clam dies, its shell opens, as does a mussel's shell Also, if a clam is buried in sediment, it can dig its way out. That is what clams do. That brings to mind a question: Why are the fossil clam shells closed?

Figure 49 – When clams die their shell opens, except if there was a global flood.

The only explanation is that the clams were buried so quickly and deeply that they could not dig their way out. The pressure of the deep layers of sediment prevented the shell from opening when the buried clam died. We do not see conditions capable of doing that today. In addition, we see fossilized closed clams globally. Whatever did this was not only massive, it was global.

The only historical event that produced the right conditions to bury clams around the world quickly and deeply was Noah's Flood.

Figure 50 – Flat layers of sediment in the Grand Canyon

Petrified Trees

Flat Sediment Layers

Location: Grand Canyon, Arizona

Notice the layers of sediment in figure 50. The boundary between layers is essentially a flat plane. If it took millions of years to deposit all these layers, as evolutionary theory states, there should be signs of erosion and vegetation growth within the layers. However, there is none. Each layer is pancaked on top of the other. If the earth is millions of years old, what we observe here, and across western North America, as well as around the world, is impossible. On the other hand, this is exactly what we would expect to see as the result of a global flood as described in the Bible.

More Global Flood Evidence: Bent Layers

Can rock such as shale or limestone be bent, without breaking it? No. Rock does not bend. That is ridiculous. Yet, in the Connecticut Valley where our dinosaur tracks come from, rock layers are bent at sharp angles. The same is seen throughout the U.S., in the Alps, in the Middle East, and around the world. How could rock be bent on a massive scale, but not be broken?

Figure 51 – Alpine mountain with massive bent sediment layers marked by the white lines.

The answer is that sedimentary rock had to have been bent while it was soft and wet, not yet hardened into rock. The means these thick, bent layers of sedimentary rock had to have been deposited

Beginner's Guide To Tracking Dinosaurs

quickly, not over time periods stretching out over millions of years. The lower layers of sediment would not have stayed soft waiting for the upper layers to be deposited. Bent rock layers are impossible based on a time frame stretched out over millions of years. However, they are exactly what we would expect to see as the result of a year long global flood.

The evidence is clear. The deep layers of sediment we see around the world were deposited over a short time… during a global Biblical flood. If you go back in time to photograph dinosaurs, do not go back more than about 5,500 years[126].(See Appendix C) That will put you in a time before the flood, when dinosaurs were abundant, but after everything came into existence. However, expect to meet people from a very different culture. People lived to be hundreds of years old, so they will have a very different perspective and culture than anything we see today. And, be careful, the closer you come to about 4,500 years ago, the chances increase that people will be very wicked.[127]

Why do I say that? We need to learn more about the flood and what God was doing.

---

[126] God's creation is about 6,000 years old.
[127] The Biblical flood was about 4500 years ago.

Petrified Trees

CHAPTER 33
THE LORD WARNED EVERYONE

"The coming of the Son of Man will be just like the days of Noah. For as in those days before the flood they were eating and drinking, marrying and giving in marriage, until the day that Noah entered the ark, and they did not understand until the flood came and took them all away; so will the coming of the Son of Man be."
— Matthew 24:37-39

Location: Somewhere on Pangea

Now the earth was corrupt in the sight of God, and the earth was filled with violence. God looked on the earth, and behold, it was corrupt.

God said to Noah, "Behold, I am about to destroy them with the earth. Make for yourself an ark of gopher wood; you shall make the ark with rooms, and shall cover it inside and out with pitch."

Then the Lord said to Noah, "Enter the ark, you and all your household, for you alone I have seen to be righteous before Me in this time."

Then the flood came upon the earth. All the high mountains were covered. All flesh that moved on the earth perished. All in whose nostrils was the breath of the spirit of life died. He blotted out every

The Lord Warned Everyone

living thing that was upon the face of the earth. Only Noah was left, together with those that were with him in the ark. -- Genesis 6 & 7 summarized

Why Did God Flood the World?

Time: 120 Years Before the Global Flood

> "Then the Lord saw that the wickedness of man was great on the earth, and that every intent of the thoughts of his heart was only evil continually. The Lord was sorry that He had made man on the earth, and He was grieved in His heart. The Lord said, 'I will blot out man whom I have created from the face of the land, from man to animals to creeping things and to birds of the sky; for I am sorry that I have made them.' But Noah found favor in the eyes of the Lord.
>
> "These are the records of the generations of Noah. Noah was a righteous man, blameless in his time; Noah walked with God. Noah became the father of three sons: Shem, Ham, and Japheth.
>
> "Now the earth was corrupt in the sight of God, and the earth was filled with violence. God looked on the earth, and behold, it was corrupt; for all flesh had corrupted their way upon the earth.
>
> "Then God said to Noah, 'The end of all flesh has come before Me; for the earth is filled with violence because of them; and behold, I am about to destroy them with the earth. Make for yourself an ark of gopher wood; you shall make the ark with rooms, and shall cover it inside and out with pitch.'" - Genesis 6:5-14

Why did God flood the world? The entire world was corrupt, evil and filled with violence.

God Warns People about What Is Coming

Time: During Construction of the Ark

It took over 100 years to build the ark. Why so long? It was big... really big. During the construction time God was using Noah, and the construction of the ark, which was sure to attract attention, to warn people about what was coming. God does this throughout history. In the book of Jonah God sends Jonah to the city of Nineveh to warn the people living there. If they do not turn away from their wicked ways, they will be destroyed. The people of Nineveh did turn away from evil and to God, and they were saved. However, in Noah's day no one listened to him.

> *"For if God did not spare angels when they sinned, but cast them into hell and committed them to pits of darkness, reserved for judgment; and did not spare the ancient world, but preserved Noah, a preacher of righteousness, with seven others, when He brought a flood upon the world of the ungodly; and if He condemned the cities of Sodom and Gomorrah to destruction by reducing them to ashes, having made them an example to those who would live ungodly lives thereafter; and if He rescued righteous Lot, oppressed by the sensual conduct of unprincipled men (for by what he saw and heard that righteous man, while living among them, felt his righteous soul tormented day after day by their lawless deeds), then the Lord knows how to rescue the godly from temptation, and to keep the unrighteous under punishment for the day of judgment, and especially those who indulge the flesh in its corrupt desires and despise authority."* - 2 Peter 2:4-10

Yes, those who disobey God will be destroyed. They will experience eternal punishment. Those who trust God to save them... who turn away from disobedience and turn to God, will be saved.

> Jesus speaking: *"For the coming of the Son of Man* [Jesus] *will be just like the days of Noah. For as in those days before the flood they were eating and drinking, marrying and giving in marriage, until the day that Noah entered the ark, and they did not understand until the flood came and took them all away; so will the coming of the Son of Man be."* - Matthew 24:37-39

Notice that Jesus speaks of the flood as a real event. To deny the global flood is to call Jesus a liar. Second, only those who listened to God's warnings, and got on the ark, were saved.

> Jesus speaking: *"And just as it happened in the days of Noah, so it will be also in the days of the Son of Man:"* [Jesus] *"they were eating, they were drinking, they were marrying, they were being given in marriage, until the day that Noah entered the ark, and the flood came and destroyed them all. It was the same as happened in the days of Lot: they were eating, they were drinking, they were buying, they were selling, they were planting, they were building; but on the*

The Lord Warned Everyone

day that Lot went out from Sodom it rained fire and brimstone from heaven and destroyed them all. It will be just the same on the day that the Son of Man is revealed." - Luke 17:26-30

The flood was real. To be saved you needed to trust God and act... go through the door of the ark. However, people went on living life as though destruction was not imminent. They ignored God's warnings and died.

Now you know why you do not want to visit the past shortly before God destroys it with a flood. The people were wicked and evil. Ever intent of their thoughts and desires were only evil continually. It does not sound like a good time to visit. Noah started building the ark about 4,500 years ago (see Appendix C). You want to arrive well before that, but not too close to the creation of the universe about 6000 years ago.

This has been a serious chapter. However, disobedience was not only a problem in Noah's day, it continues today. Your sin is a serious matter with eternal consequences. We shouldn't leave this topic without fully understanding the situation and the only solution.

CHAPTER 34
2ND PETER 2:4-6

Peter Is Warning Us

Peter gives three examples showing how God deals with evil:

"For if God did not spare angels when they sinned, but cast them into hell and committed them to pits of darkness, reserved for judgment; and did not spare the ancient world, but preserved Noah, a preacher of righteousness, with seven others, when He brought a flood upon the world of the ungodly; and if He condemned the cities of Sodom and Gomorrah to destruction by reducing them to ashes, having made them an example to those who would live ungodly lives thereafter;"

(1) Peter points out that even angels, if they disobey God, will be cast into hell and eternal punishment. Evil is defined as disobeying God. Anyone who does not obey God perfectly is facing judgment and eternity in the lake of fire.

(2) Next Peter points out that the entire world (and that means everyone) is subject to God's judgment. Majority rule does not determine what is right and wrong, no matter how large the majority, even if it is the entire world. God alone determines what is right and what is evil, and His criteria never changes. At the time of the global flood everyone, except for the eight people who went through the door of the ark, perished. Everyone turned away from God, except Noah and His family.

(3) The third example is that of Sodom and Gomorrah. These cities had reached a point of being totally wicked, as illustrated in Genesis 19:5 & 9-10:

The men of Sodom, both young and old, all the people from every quarter, meaning the entire population...

> *"called to Lot and said to him, 'Where are the men who came to you tonight? Bring them out to us that we may have relations with them." Lot refused to send out the two men (who were actually angels). But the crowd outside Lot's house did not give up, "But they said, 'Stand aside.' Furthermore, they said, 'This one came in as an alien, and already he is acting like a judge; now we will treat you worse than them.' So they pressed hard against Lot and came near to break the door. But the men (the angels) reached out their hands and brought Lot into the house with them, and shut the door."*

God explains why He Destroyed Sodom and Gomorrah...

God is using these cities as examples for everyone in the future, including us today. There is no doubt they were wicked. The entire population, except for Lot and his family, were engaged in homosexuality, to the point of using violence to satisfy their sexual desires. However, what is surprising is God's patience in not immediately bringing judgment. The world today deserves the punishment Sodom and Gomorrah received. Yet today God is being patient. Withholding His judgment until the full number of those whom He has chosen are saved. However, so that we would know judgment is certain, He has givens us Sodom and Gomorrah as an example.

That is the point Peter is making. Judgment is certain. Disobeying God WILL have consequences. There will be justice. Angels who disobey God cannot escape God's justice. Even if it is the entire world disobeying God, judgment is coming. Punishment is sure, complete, and appropriate as we saw in Sodom and Gomorrah.

The message is clear. There will be judgment. Punishment for breaking God's laws is guaranteed.

Beginner's Guide To Tracking Dinosaurs

2 Peter 2:7-8

"and if He rescued righteous Lot, oppressed by the sensual conduct of unprincipled men (for by what he saw and heard that righteous man, while living among them, felt his righteous soul tormented day after day by their lawless deeds),"

Yes, judgment is coming, but then Peter points out there is hope. God will rescue some... those who are righteous. Lot was a righteous man, believing God and trusting Him. Yet, he lived in an evil city, and was tormented by the lawlessness all around him. He longed to be with people who obeyed God... he longed for God's righteousness... and despaired because all of those around him ignored God.

2 Peter 2:9-10

"then the Lord knows how to rescue the godly from a trial, and to keep the unrighteous under punishment for the day of judgment, and especially those who indulge the flesh in its corrupt passion and despise authority."

As bad as Sodom and Gomorrah were, God rescues Lot and his family from the coming judgment. We can trust that God has the power, ability, and authority to rescue us from His judgment. There is no one alive today who is any better than the people who were living in Sodom.and Gomorrah. We all face God's justice and the sure penalty of the eternal lake of fire. We have been clearly warned that judgment is coming. The only salvation is to trust in Jesus Christ.

God will rescue those who believe and trust in the righteousness of Jesus to save them. He did it 2000 years ago when He died on the cross paying the penalty we owe for disobeying God. This gift is available to you, if you want it. Repent, turn away from disobedience and trust that Jesus paid the penalty you have earned for sin (disobeying God)... paid it IN FULL.

2nd Peter 2:4-6

CHAPTER 35
THE DOOR

About 4,500 years ago, the world was filled with wickedness. The...

"Lord saw that the wickedness of man was great on the earth, and that every intent of the thoughts of his heart was only evil continually." - Genesis 6:5

God, through Noah, a preacher of righteousness, warned the world of the coming judgment. The entire world would be destroyed and everyone would perish, EXCEPT those who went through the door of the ark. People needed to trust what God was telling them, turn away from their unbelief, and obey God by going through the door and getting on the ark.

It Was Easy.
Believe God.
Go Through the Door and Be Saved

The only ones who listened and obeyed were Noah's family. There was plenty of room on the ark. It was huge. It required little physical effort. Just walk up the ramp. However, no one else went through the door... and they died.

Today we have the same choice. The door into the ark foreshadows Jesus Christ. He is the door. God has warned us. Judgment is

Was There A Roman Census?

coming. The only way to be saved is to go through Jesus Christ. Trust Jesus (God). Turn away from the ways of the world, and obey God. Trust that Jesus will save you from God's judgment. He is the only way.

> *"It is appointed for men to die once and after this comes judgment."*
> - Hebrews 9:27

We all will die. You know judgment is coming.

> *"...those who do not know God and to those who do not obey the gospel of our Lord Jesus. These will pay the penalty of eternal destruction, away from the presence of the Lord."* - 2 Thessalonians 1:8b-9a

To understand what it means to be *"away from the presence of the Lord,"* you need to understand that everything good comes from God. Without God you have nothing good. Even those who totally reject God today, are not away from the Lord. Even an atheist is still receiving good things from God. God is being patient, and is giving good things to all of His image bearers, including you, who are alive today. However, when you die that ends. If you have not gone through the door that is Jesus Christ, you will be away from the presence of the Lord. That means you will have nothing good. Nothing. A cool drink of water, relief from pain, and friends are all good. You will not have them. Even light and having someone… anyone to talk to is good. You will not have them. That is why it is called hell. There is NOTHING good. If you chose to reject Jesus (God), that is what you will get for eternity never ending, You will be completely separated from Him.

> *"He who does not believe has been judged already, because he has not believed in the name of the only begotten Son of God."* - John 3:18

This is true. However, let's step back and look at the first part of the verse:

Beginner's Guide To Tracking Dinosaurs

"He who believes in Him is not judged; he who does not believe has been judged already, because he has not believed in the name of the only begotten Son of God."

He who believes in Him is not judged;

If you believe in Jesus, you are saved from God's judgment. Jesus takes your punishment on himself. This does not mean believing God is real. The demons believe that and tremble (James 2:19). So what do you need to believe?

But these" [referring to the Gospel of John] *"have been written so that you may believe that Jesus is the Christ, the Son of God; and that believing you may have life in His name."* - John 20:31

You need to believe Jesus is your Savior. That He is the one who will save you from the consequences of your rebellion against God. Trust Jesus. Turn away from disobeying God.

Was There A Roman Census?

CHAPTER 36
IT IS FINISHED!

Figure 52 – the cross is empty. It is finished.

Notice that the center cross is empty. Jesus is not on the cross. That is important. Jesus is no longer on the cross; His work on the cross is finished.

Jesus's last words, as He was hanging on the cross, were *"It is finished."*

> "Therefore when Jesus had received the sour wine, He said, 'It is finished!' And He bowed His head and gave up His spirit." - John 19:30

It Is Finished

Jesus was saying that what He had come to earth to do was finished. There was no more to be done. He had lived a perfect life as a man. He taught His followers. And, as He was dying physically on the cross, He paid the penalty for sin for everyone who would be saved...past, present and future. There was nothing more to do. The penalty for sin had been paid in full.

Jesus did it all. It is finished.

There is nothing for you to do, nor is there anything you can do. Believe this is true. Repent. Turn away from disobeying God. Do as God has commanded and trust Jesus as your Savior from God's punishment for sin. Read His word in the Bible, and do what He says.

> *"For I delivered to you as of first importance what I also received: that Christ died for our sins in accordance with the Scriptures, that he was buried, that he was raised on the third day in accordance with the Scriptures."* – 1 Corinthians 15:3-4

Yes, there is life after your physical death. The story does not end on the cross. On the third day Jesus Christ rose from the dead, proving that everything He said and promised is true! With Jesus as your Savior, death is the beginning, not the end. Praise God!

APPENDIX A
"TEN QUESTIONS

In this appendix, I will answer ten of the most common creation related questions. These questions are on a sign in our museum, with some very short answers, sometimes just one word. We will go into a little more depth here. If you would like more information, each answer has a link to more detail on our SciencePastor.com web site.

(1) Where did Cain get his wife?
www.AJ83.com/cainswife

Cain married his sister. Why do we think that is disgusting? Because it is just not done. Marrying a close relative means both people have many of the same mutations. This is called inbreeding and results in serious mutations and medical problems for the children. However, because they had essentially no mutations, the children of Cain and his wife would be fine.

(2) Can Christians believe in evolution?
www.SciencePastor.com/wrongorder

They can. Believing that God creating everything from nothing is not a requirement for salvation, but evolution is incompatible with the Bible. One of the biggest problems Christians should have with evolution is that natural selection drives evolution, and natural selection works through death. The better fit survive and the weak die off. If humans evolved from apes, that means death came before Adam, and believing that is a huge problem. Believing death came before Adam means rejecting a plain reading of scripture, as well as rejecting the gospel.

(3) Doesn't carbon dating prove the earth is very old?
www.SciencePastor.com/carbon14

No. It is scientifically impossible because carbon dating is only good for short time durations... tens of thousands of years not millions of years. Other types of radioactive dating are used for long ages. However, that does not help. Those dating methods are based on assumptions that result in these types of dating methods being unreliable and highly inaccurate.

(4) How do dinosaurs fit in the Bible?
www.AJ83.com/dragon

The Bible does not have a problem with dinosaurs. They are mentioned several times However, the Bible is not a book about dinosaurs. The purpose of the Bible is to inform us about our condition, who God is, and what He has done to deal with our condition. The Bible was not written to tell us about dinosaurs. However, for example, in the course of describing God and what He created, dinosaurs are mentioned in Job 40.

God created dinosaurs on day six of creation when he created the land animals, the same day he created humanity. Dinosaurs are part of God's creation and are mentioned at times in the Bible when it talks about God's creation.

(5) Haven't scientists proven the earth is billions of years old? – www.SciencePastor.com/young

Evolution requires the earth to be billions of years old. If it were any younger, there would not be enough time for evolution to happen. It is not that the evidence shows the earth to be old, it's that evolution falls apart if the earth in not billions of years old.

Beginner's Guide To Tracking Dinosaurs

The claim is that radioactive dating shows the earth to be old. However, the radioactive dating methods are based on assumptions designed to give the desired answers, and all evidence to the contrary is ignored.

(5) How did Noah get all the animals on the ark?
www.SciencePastor.com/ark

Easily. There was plenty of room. If you get a chance, visit the Ark Encounter in Kentucky and see for yourself.

God did not have to bring the fully-grown dinosaurs. It would make sense to bring the smaller, young dinosaurs. They would take up less space, eat less, and produce less waste. Most of the dinosaur reproductions in our museum are life-size juveniles.

(7) Wasn't there a gap between the first two verses of Genesis? - www.AJ83.com/gap

No gap. The idea that there is a time gap of billions of years between the first two verses of Genesis is an idea created to accommodate evolution. It is not supported by evolution-based science nor by scripture. For example Exodus 20:11 states: *"In six days, the LORD made heaven and earth, the sea, and all that is in them."* This is a plain statement by God that He made everything in six, ordinary, 24-hour days. And Romans 5:12 states, *"by one man sin entered into the world, and death by sin."* However, based on the Gap Theory God is wrong to say this. There was actually hundreds of millions of years of death before Adam. The Gap Theory does not make sense.

(8) Don't skulls show evolution from ape to human?
www.AJ83.com/tree

Nope. Fossils identified based on evolutionary theory as being in the human lineage can be placed into two categories: fully human and fully ape. The human skulls are fully modern human. Although they may have pathologies or genetic-based differences, for example as the result of inbreeding, they all fit within normal human variation. The non-human skulls are ape skulls. Claims they are human ancestors are based on incomplete fossils or body fossils. Ape and human fossils are often found mixed together, resulting in skeletons that are

Appendix A: Ten Questions

part human body fossils and part ape fossils, brought together based on wishful thinking.

(9) Are the days of creation ordinary days?
www.SciencePastor.com/day

Yes, they are six 24-hour days. Hebrew scholars agree that Genesis is written as a historical narrative, meaning it is written to report real historical events. When Genesis uses the word "day" in chapter one, it means a 24-hour day. The context makes this very clear. The days being are numbered. Day one. Day two. And so on. When days are numbered in the Bible, they are always 24-hour days. The context also includes the phrase "evening and morning." That is a phrase that defines a 24-hour day.

(10) Where did the races come from?
www.AJ83.com/race

The races come from the eight people on the ark. Every human alive today comes from Noah and his wife, their three sons and their wives. All eight of them were on the ark. So we are all related... EVREY ONE of us. We have cultural differences, but we are ALL one race. People were divided when God confused the languages at Babel. Speaking different languages people could not understand each other. The result was division, and humanity spread across the globe, the people of each language group seeking a place they could make their own.

APPENDIX B
THE NASH DINOSAUR TRACK QUARRY

How did we find our dinosaur tracks? It was easy. We went to Nash's Dinosaur Track Quarry. Located in Granby, MA, just one mile from where the first dinosaur track was discovered on the farm of Pliny Moody. The Nash Dinosaur Track Quarry was in operation for 80 years, 1939 through 2019. It is now closed.

In 1933 Carlton Nash discovered an outcrop of dinosaur tracks just off Aldrich street in Granby. Three years later in 1939 the owner of the property was planning to dynamite the rock to produce flagstones. Carlton was able to purchase 1-3/4 acres containing the dinosaur footprint site, just in time. Over the years pioneering paleontologists visited the quarry such as great the American dinosaur hunters Barnum Brown and R.T. Bird, and more recently Roy Chapman Andrews, Jim Jensen, and Jack Horner.

Carlton Nash passed away in 1997 at the age of 82. His son Kornell Nash then took over the operation of the quarry and store. Kornell passed away in 2019 and the quarry is now closed.

How Were Tracks Quarried?

The type of rock in the quarry is shale, which is a fined grained sedimentary rock.

The Nash Dinosaur Track Quarry

Dinosaur tracks were quarried by peeling off the layers of shale. This is done by finding a horizontal crack (there are many – there are cracks where there is mica) and lightly tapping dinner knives into the crack. The dinner knives are used as wedges to slowly and gently open up the crack. See figure 53

As the crack gets bigger, metal carpenter's rulers were then tapped into the growing crack to continue to enlarge it.

Figure 53 – Cracking layers of shale to reveal dinosaur tracks

As the crack grew still larger, pry bars were gently and slowly tapped into the crack, enlarging it further. Once the slate slab was breaking free, additional pry bars were sometimes used to fully break the slab free and lift it up. The entire operation must be done gently and slowly.

Once the slab was lifted up, Kornell could take a look to see if there were any dinosaur tracks. There is no way to tell ahead of time what is inside the rock. Only after it has been split and the top piece is lifted does the interior of the rock reveal its secrets.

Quarrying dinosaur tracks is slow, hard work, and sometimes after an hour of work all you have is... a piece of rock. Sometimes a slab breaks in two, right in the middle of what would have been a great dinosaur track. And sometimes there is a good dinosaur track or maybe two or three!

However, your job is not done. At times, once the rock is cracked open faint traces are seen that indicate something better may be inside the piece of rock. That means starting over with the dinner knives to further split the shale slab that was just pried up.

Beginner's Guide To Tracking Dinosaurs

Once good quality dinosaur tracks are found (not all tracks are good quality), they need to be cut out of the slab to provide a manageable and saleable size rock. The final step was to stain the track to make it easier to see.

I should note that the quarry was not a "you pick" quarry. For an admission fee of $3 visitors were welcome to go into the quarry. However, the actual quarrying of the dinosaur tracks was done by people who knew what they were doing. It is much easier to destroy a rock than to get it out of the ground in one piece with tracks on it.

Something Odd... Mud Cracks

When mud quickly hardens in the sun the result is usually mud cracks. As the mud dries the overall volume of the mud decreases, resulting in cracks. The shape of mud cracks formed in the sun will vary depending on how many times the mud was wetted and dried.

Mud cracks can also form under water. As sediment builds up underwater the weight of the sediment will squeeze the water out of the lower layers of sediment. The mud shrinks and cracks form. Underwater mud cracks can also form as a result of changes in the salinity of the water. Mud cracks formed underwater have a different pattern than those formed in the sun.

Dinosaur tracks from the Connecticut River Valley in Massachusetts give us a unique opportunity to study the relationship of dinosaur tracks and mud cracks. The local conditions are said to have been that of a shallow muddy lake shoreline, with annual water level fluctuations and a high sedimentation rate. The result was successive episodes of burial that preserved dinosaur footprints, water ripples, raindrop impressions, and mud cracks... but the mud cracks are only seen in certain locations. That should get us thinking, and asking, why?

Why Mud Cracks There and Not Here?

Our dinosaur tracks come from the Nash Quarry, about two miles east of the Connecticut River. Notice on the map (figure 54) that the Connecticut River is just a short distance east of the Mount Tom range. Dinosaur tracks, along with mud cracks are found between the river and the Mount Tom range. However, mud cracks are

The Nash Dinosaur Track Quarry

not seen at the Nash quarry, nor at any site I have seen east of the river. The question is, why?

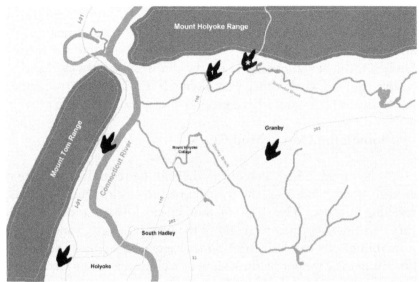

Figure 54 - The Nash Quarry is marked by a Dinosaur silhouette with an asterisk just south of the Mt. Holyoke Range. The track marked as #1 is where the first dinosaur tracks were found in 1803. Other track silhouettes mark publically known sites where dinosaur tracks have been found.

The Geology of the Connecticut River Valley

The Connecticut River Valley is a half-graben (figure 55) rift valley in what is geologically called the Holyoke Basin. The pivot point, and the river, are on the west side of the valley at the Mount Tom Range. The east side of the valley sank, dropping thousands of feet. The west edge stayed in place, acting as a hinge point. Several layers of sediment and lava flows (flood basalt) filled the valley as it sank on the east. The sediment is very deep in the east and thin in the west (see figure 56).

The evolutionary assumption is that the half-graben formed and filled with sediment over a long period of time, several million years. However, what if it formed in about a year during Noah's Flood. The sediment and lava would have been deposited quickly. The result would be that the sediment along the western edge, where the layers are thin and mud cracks are found, would be very warm. The heat from the lava flows would have quickly dried the sediment, not the sun. While just a short distance to the east, the lava was buried too deeply and quickly to warm the surface. And thus no mud cracks are found there.

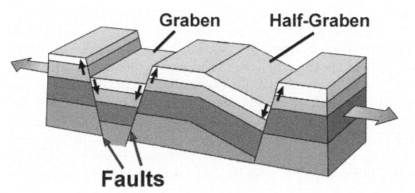

Figure 55 – The Connecticut River Valley is a half graben rift valley. The land sank on the east side, with mountains rising up at the hinge point.

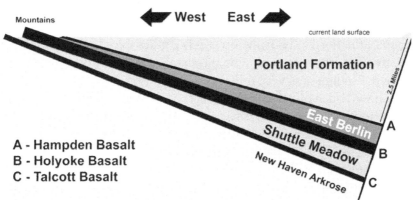

A - Hampden Basalt
B - Holyoke Basalt
C - Talcott Basalt

Figure 56 – The Mt. Tom Range and the Connecticut River are on the far west side of the half graben. The black layers are flood basalt lava flows. They flowed over a flat surface that continually sank on the east side, tilting the sediment and lava flows.

The result would be dinosaur tracks and mud cracks along the western edge of the valley, but mud cracks would be rare elsewhere.

The Nash Dinosaur Track Quarry

MORE ON THE HOLYOKE BASIN GEOLOGY
Geological Cross-Section of the Valley

The Holyoke Basin formed as the continents broke apart. The term "half-graben" means that only one side of the valley sank, while the other side remained stationary, serving as a pivot point.

The New Haven Arkrose (sandstone) was deposited as a flat layer of sediment before the valley started to form. As the eastern edge started sinking, the valley filled with additional sediment. The layers of sediment tilted to the east as the eastern edge of the valley continued to sink. New sediment continued to be added to the valley, with the major divisions named, Shuttle Meadow, East Berlin and the Portland Formation. In addition, lava eruptions spread vast sheets of flood basalts across the new valley. When lava hardens to rock it is called basalt. There are three major layers of flood basalt in the valley, the Talcott Basalt, Holyoke Basalt, and Hampden Basalt. These lava flows are part of what is thought to be the largest lava flow on Earth, the Central Atlantic Magmatic Province (CAMP). The flood basalt was flat when deposited, as was the sediment. They became tilted as the eastern edge of the valley continued to sink.

Figure 56 is a simplistic sketch, but it provides an overall idea of the geology of the valley. Notice the depth of the sediment. At its deepest the Portland Formation is 2-1/2 miles thick in the east. These are massive layers of sediment and basalt. However, on the western edge the sediment is very thin.

Based on evolutionary thinking the layers of sediment and flood basalt took millions of years to accumulate. However, using a Biblical time scale the valley would have formed and filled with sediment during the year of Noah's Flood. The hot flood basalts would have been quickly covered with wet sediment. And where the sediment was thin, along the western edge of the valley, between the basalt mountains of the Mount Tom Range and where the river is now located, the heat from the flood basalt would have quickly dried the sediment leaving mud cracks. No sun required.

When a Biblical perspective is applied to what is observed, it all starts to make sense.

APPENDIX C
AGE OF THE EARTH

The earth was created about 6,000 years ago. That claim is dramatically different from the billions of years claimed by evolution. Such a huge difference should make it easy to distinguish one from the other when we look at the evidence.

Why Do I Say the Earth is 6000 Years Old?

Why do I say the earth is about 6,000 years old? The Bible does not make any direct claims about the earth being young (6,000) or old (billions of years). However, the Bible infers the earth is young and it assumes that we will believe to be true all that the Bible asserts to be true in a plain, straight-forward reading[128].

God gave us the Bible to reveal Himself to us as the creator (and owner) of us and the universe. It explains the situation we are in as sinners who disobey God. The Old Testament shows that no matter how much we desire it, nor how hard we try, we are not good. We will always disobey God and the consequence is death. The Old Testament also foreshadows God's solution, which is revealed in full in the New Testament. The cross. On the cross Jesus (God) takes on Himself the full punishment we deserve for disobeying our Creator. If we believe, we will be saved from God's punishment, just as Noah and his family were saved from the flood.

---

[128] Such as the information in the genealogies in the Bible.

Image Credits

In giving us our history, God gives us genealogies that are important in showing we all came from Adam, and more importantly that Jesus came from Adam and from Abraham (and the line of king David). From these historical facts we can calculate the age of the earth.[129]

Father	Son	Age at Birth	Total Years	
Adam	Seth	130	130	Genesis 5
Seth	Enosh	105	235	
Enosh	Kenan	90	325	
Kenan	Mahalel	70	395	
Mahalel	Jared	65	460	
Jared	Enoch	162	622	
Enoch	Methuselah	65	687	
Methuselah	Lamech	187	874	
Lamech	Noah	182	1056	
Noah	Flood	600	1656	Gen. 7:11
Flood	Arphaxad	2	1658	Genesis 11
Arphaxad	Shelah	35	1693	
Shelah	Eber	30	1723	
Eber	Peleg	34	1757	
Peleg	Reu	30	1787	
Reu	Serug	32	1819	
Serug	Nahor	30	1849	
Nahor	Terah	29	1878	
Terah	Abram	130	2008	
Abraham	Isaac	100	2108	Gen. 21:5
Isaac	Jacob	60	2168	Gen. 25:26
EVENT	**EVENT**	**TIME**		
Jacob	Egypt	130	2298	Gen. 47:9
Jacob in Egypt	Exodus	430	2728	Ex. 12:40
Exodus	Temple begun	480	3208	1 Kings 6:1
Temple	Exile	345	3553	

This brings us to the time of the kings in Judah and Israel, for

---

[129] https://creation.com/6000-years

which we have historical records that bring us up to today. Adding up the dates gives us an age for the earth of about 6,150, which is commonly expressed as about 6,000 years.

What about Billions of Years?

The reason for the earth to be billions of years old is because that is what evolution requires. Without billions of years, it is impossible for the Big Bang, random mutations, and natural selection to assemble everything that we see today. In fact, even with billions of years it is still impossible, but billions is as much as they can come up with.

As I have mentioned previously, the unbreakable rule is that all of science must agree with evolutionary theory, and not do anything that casts any doubt in any way on evolution. That is an unbreakable "law" and that requires that facts be ignored and billions of years be proclaimed.

Scientific Facts Supporting Billions of Years

It always comes down to radiometric dating. Radioactive materials generally decay at a certain, known rate. We can very accurately measure radioactive materials and, based on numerous assumptions, use their ratios to calculate how long the decay process has been taking place. This gives us the "age" of the material containing the radioactive materials.

The fly in the ointment is the word "assume." Assumptions are made so that the results of radiometric dating ALWAYS come out to be in agreement with evolutionary thinking, even if the data from radiometric dating does not. That is right, it does not matter what the actual data results are, the reported results of radiometric dating will always support evolutionary theory.

> "What happens when multiple dating methods agree on an apparent age that conflicts with the ape-to-man story? In such cases, the paradigm will consistently take precedence over the data."[130]

---

[130] Christopher Rupe and Dr. John Sanford, "Bones of Contention," (2019) page 287

> "The KBS Tuff [dating] controversy reveals that what determines the age of hominin bones is not the actual dating methods, but rather the researcher's *a priori* commitment to a particular model of hominin evolution."[131]

> "Contrary to the impression that we are given, radiometric dating does not prove that the Earth is millions of years old. The vast age has simply been assumed. The calculated radiometric 'ages' depend on the assumptions that are made. The results are only accepted if they agree with what is already believed. The only foolproof method for determining the age of something is based on eyewitness reports and a written record. We have both in the Bible."[132]

The problems with radiometric dating become glaringly obvious when it is used to date rocks of known ages, for example rocks from volcanic eruptions that have been observed and recorded in history. For example, using potassium-argon dating, rocks from Mt. St. Helens (May 1980 eruption) were dated to be from 350,000 to 2.8 million years old[133]. Multiple samples from lava flows from Mount Ngauruhoe in New Zealand, resulting from eruptions in 1949, 1954, and 1975 were dated. One sample was dated at 270,000 years, the rest had ages in the millions of years. Repeat testing on two samples resulted in the same results.[134]

As you can see there is a problem with the accuracy and reliability of radiometric dating. But, what about other methods of radioactive dating, such as fission track dating? It is no better.

> "Different grains within the same pumice sample gave different fission track ages. Some yielded an average age of 2.44 million years, whereas others ranged from 290 million years old to 380 million years old! How could samples taken from the same eruption event (the KBS Tuff) result in such widely discrepant ages."[135]

If I was traveling back in time, I would not bet my life by trusting

---

[131] Christopher Rupe and Dr. John Sanford, "Bones of Contention," (2019) page 293
[132] Dr. Tas Walker, "The way it really is: little-known facts about radiometric dating " Creation 24, (Sept. 2002)- https://tinyurl.com/y2y595sm
[133] Dr. Tas Walker, "Learning the Lessons of Mout St. Helens," - https://creation.com/lessons-from-mount-st-helens
[134] Dr. Andrew Snelling, Radioactive 'Datign' Failure, Creation Ex Nihilo, December 1999, https://creation.com/radioactive-dating-failure
[135] Christopher Rupe and Dr. John Sanford, "Bones of Contention," (2019) page 294

Beginner's Guide To Tracking Dinosaurs

radioactive dating methods. Going back in time to a point before anything existed would surely result in my no longer existing. What would you do?

Image Credits

Image Credits

Note: the CC License may be read here: https://creativecommons.org/licenses/by-sa/3.0/deed.en

Figure 1: Image credit: AdmiralHood (Wikki Commons), modified to combine two images into a single image and add text, CC License.

Figure 2: Photo: Coelophysis photographed in the Dickinson (ND) Museum Center. Dilophosaurus photographed in Dinosaur State Park Museum (Rocky Hill, CT). Both photos and editing are by the author.

Figure 3: Image credit: KoprX (Wikki Commons), modified to make legend readable and to add title, CC License.

Figure 4: Author photograph

Figure 5: Plazak at English Wikipedia (Wikki Commons), image cropped, CC license

Figure 6-8: Author photographs and graphics

Figure 9-11: Kornell Nash drawings. Used with permission.

Figures 12-27: Author photos and graphics

Figures 31-33: Images from Michael Oard's book "Dinosaur Challenges and Mysteries," used with permission.

Figures 34-35: Author photos and graphics

Figure 36: Image from Michael Oard's book "Dinosaur Challenges and Mysteries," used with permission.

Figure 37-Author photo and graphics

Figure 38: Public domain with author modifications

Image Credits

Figure 39: Author photo and graphics

Figure 40: Stock photo`

Figure 41-49: Author photos and graphics

Figure 50: Stock photo
Figure-51-52: Stock photo with author graphics

Figure 53-56: Author photos and graphics

Subject Index

1 Corinthians 15:3-4 - 184
2 Peter 2:4-10 - 172-173
2 Peter 2:4-6 - 175-177
2 Thessalonians 1;8b-9a - 180
Ahlquist, Dr. Jon 87
Anchisauripus 16
Anomoepus 18
Antibiotic resistance 102
Archaeopteryx 85, 89-91, 94
Archaeopteryx, bird features 90
Archaeopteryx, dinosaur features 89-90
Ark, how did animals all fit 187
Australopithicus afarensis 147-150
Batrachopus 18
BEDS 56-60, 75
Bible, and science 136
Bible, contradicts science 138-139
Bible, dinosaurs 186
Bible, humanist objections 137-139
Bible, miracles 137-138
Bible, or evolution 152-153
Bird evolution 83-87, 97-100
Bird evolution evidence 84, 89-90
Bird phylogeny 86-87
Bird, hip structure 99-100
Bird, lungs 97-98
Bird, wing movement 98-99
Briefly Exposed Diluvial Sediments 56-60, 75

Cain's wife 185
Carbon dating, 62, 126, 159-161
Carbon dating, age of the earth 186
Carbon dating, dinosaur bones 161
Carbon dating, tracks 159-161
Carnivores dominate 41, 63, 64, 66
Carnivorous dinosaurs 60
Causality, law of 141-145
Ceolosaurus 6
Chimpanzee DNA 101-102, 115-117
Chinese characters 52-53
Clams, evidence for flood 166-167
Coalified wood 60
Coelophysis 7
Crete footprints 156-157
Cross, the 183-184
Dating rocks.. 195-198
Devolution 102, 119-120, 126
Dilophosaurus 7
Dinosaur to Bird evolution 83-84
Dinosaur, egg clutches 67-68
Dinosaur, egg preservation 70-71
Dinosaur, egg shell protein 72
Dinosaur, eggs 57-60, 67-78
Dinosaur, nests 67-69
Dinosaur, numbering toes 29-30
Dinosaur, ornithopod eggs 68

Subject Index

Dinosaur, size 33-34
Dinosaur, speed 35-36
Dinosaur, theropod eggs 68
Dinosaurs, as food 49-50
Dinosaurs, carbon dating 161
Dinosaurs, categories 6
Dinosaurs, food source 63
Dinosaurs, poor swimmers 64
Dinosaurs, swimming 20, 57, 59
Dinosaurs, walking 59
DNA 83, 101, 115-120
DNA scaffolding 117
DNA, antimalarial mutations 126
DNA, loss of information 118
DNA, preprogrammed mutations 119
Earth, age of 186-187, 195-198
Egg, preservation summary 74-75
Egg clutches 67-69
Egg shell protein 72
Eggs 67-78
Eggs, flood evidence 74-76
Eggs, fossilization today 73
Eggs, multiple shells 71
Eggs, not hatched 71-72
Eggs, pathological 70-71
Eggs, preservation 70-71
Eggs, rapid fossilization 73-74
Eggs, shape 68
Eubrontes 5, 7, 16, 18, 39
Evolution, and Christians 185-186
Evolution, ape to human 187
Evolution, definition 105, 109-113
Evolution, definition, 1840 - 109
Evolution, definition, 1942 110-111
Evolution, equivocation 106, 112-113
Evolution, fact check 101
Evolution, finches 107-108
Evolution, fossil record 124-126
Evolution, general theory 112
Evolution, genetic proof 116
Evolution, human 129-133
Evolution, myths 105-108
Evolution, observing 103-104
Evolution, proclaiming 127

Evolution, proof 123-124
Evolution, skulls 187
Evolution, special theory 112
Evolution, speciation 107-108
Evolution, upright walking 127
Feathers 84, 90, 94-95
Fission track dating..198
Flat bedding planes 41, 59, 62, 64
Flood evidence, clams 66-167
Flood evidence, sediment 167-168
Flood evidence, trees 163-166
Flood legends 50-52
Flood, animals on the ark 187
Flood, global 20, 50, 52, 56-60, 61, 77, 164-169, 173, 175
Fossil, record 107
Fossils, dating failures 126
Fossils, human 155-157
Fossils, mixed up bones 129-133
Gap Theory 187
General Theory of Evolution 112
Genesis 1:1-10 - ix
Genesis 1:26-27 - 4
Genesis 19:5 & 9-10 - 176
Genesis 6 & 7 - 171
Genesis 6:5- 179
Genesis, ordinary days 188
Gigandipus 17
Global Flood 20, 50, 52, 56-60, 61, 77, 164-169, 173, 175
Global flood, warnings 171-173
God, creator 142-145
God, judgment 177
God, revealed through creation 144
God, revealed through His word 145
God, separated from 180
God, uncreated creator 145
God, who made 141-145
Grallator 5, 7, 16
Half graben 192-193
Hebrews 9:27 - 180
Holyoke Basic Geology 194
Homo erectus 125, 132-133
Homo floresiensis 131

Beginner's Guide To Tracking Dinosaurs

Homo habilis 125, 130-131
Human fossils 155-157
Human races 188
Human-Chimpanzee DNA 101 115-117
It is Finished 183-184
Jesus, believing 181
Jesus, the cross 183-184
Jesus, the door 179-181
Jesus, trusting 135-139
John 19:30 - 183-184
John 20:31 - 181
Kerkut, G.A. 112
Laetoli footprints 155-157
Lenski 108
Lucy 125, 147-150
Lucy- discovery of 149-150
Lucy, human ancestor 148
Lucy, mixed bones 149
Lucy, saved? 151-153
Malaria 126
Matthew 24:37-39- 1
Mica 12
Microraptor 93-96
Microraptor, evidence 95-96
Mud cracks 191-193
Mutations, beneficial 118-119, 126
Mutations, preprogrammed 119
Mutations, random 118-120
Nash Dinosaur Track Quarry 189-194
Oard, Michael 56-60, 73
Ornithischian 6
Ornithopod 5, 8, 21, 29, 68
Ornithopod, identifying 25-28
Otozoum 17
Overprints 14, 46
Petrified trees 163-166
Phylogeny 86
Presuppositions 79-81
Presuppositions, evolution 80-81
Pubis 6, 100
Races, origin of 188
Radiometric dating 195-198
Raindrops, preservation 47-48, 55
Ripples, fossil 38, 63
Rock, bent 168

Romans 1:28 - v
Saurischia 6
Sauropods 8
Sediment, flat 167-168
Sickle-cell anemia 120
Sodom and Gomorrah 176-177
Special Theory of Evolution 112
Speciation 103-104, 112-113
Supersaurus 6
T-Rex 6, 79
Theropod 5, 29, 84, 97
Theropod, identifying 21-24
Theropod, tracks 7, 19, 23
Track, preservation 42-47, 57-60 61-62
Tracks, carbon dating 159-161
Tracks, ceratopsian 19-20
Tracks, flood evidence 65-66
Tracks, impressed 12
Tracks, left or right foot 31-32
Tracks, marine environment 60
Tracks, mud cracks 191-193
Tracks, Naming 8, 15
Tracks, Nash Quarry 189-194
Tracks, no change over time 63
Tracks, Ornithopod 8, 25-28
Tracks, overprints 14
Tracks, present day 61
Tracks, preservation 55
Tracks, quarrying 189-190
Tracks, raised 12, 32
Tracks, Sauropod 9, 19
Tracks, sediment filling 46
Tracks, splitting 12
Tracks, stone color 62-63
Tracks, Theropod 7, 21-24
Tracks, Triceratops 19
Tracks, true tracks 12, 13, 46
Tracks, underprints 13, 45
Tracks, with ripples 63
Tracksites, carnivorous dinosaurs 60
Tracksites, flat bedding planes 59, 62
Tracksites, marine environment 64
Tracksites, vegetation 41, 59, 62
Trackways 5, 64
True Print 12, 13, 46

Subject Index

Truth, opposition to 157
Truth, suppression 159-161
Turtles all the way down 143
Underprints 13, 45
Universe, possible causes 143-144

ABOUT THE AUTHOR

Steve is a retired pastor and has been the executive director of the Move to Assurance (MTA) ministry since 2000. MTA produces apologetic videos and books, and is involved in street evangelism, outreach, and apologetics ministries.
Some of the MTA web sites include:

www.911Christ.com
www.DinosaurTracker.com
www.MTAbible.com
www.MoveToAssurance.org
www.DinosaursForJesus.com
www.SciencePastor.com
www.HaystackRock.org

MTA's YouTube Channel: www.tinyurl.com/yc83ddgm
Facebook: www.facebook.com/sciencepastor

About the Author

Some of the other books by Steve Hudgik available on Amazon.com

Mrs. Bartlett and Her Class
At the Metropolitan Tabernacle

The biography of an amazing and inspirational women who taught at Spurgeon's church. She was a prayer warrior and evangelist.
(By her son Edward Bartlett. Notes by Steve Hudgik)

RUN! It's Jesus Calling

Why you should throw away your Copy of the *Jesus Calling* devotional book.

The Presence of God

A commentary on the Book of Esther, the only book in the Bible that does not mention God.

Happy Are The...

Discovering the blessings of God and the Road to salvation in the Beatitudes

Sarah Young's Jesus Always Exposed

Shinning the light of scripture on the *Jesus Always* Devotional

Answers to 120 Humanist Accusations Against the Bible

This two volume set answers 180 humanist accusation that attempt to show the Bible has errors, contradictions, false prophecies, and that God is Cruel

Made in the USA
Columbia, SC
13 July 2021